Five to Seven

Five to Seven

The Story of a 1920s Childhood

Diana Noel

with illustrations by Eric Stemp

Collins
14 St James's Place
London

William Collins Sons & Co Ltd
London · Glasgow · Sydney · Auckland
Toronto · Johannesburg

First published 1978

© Diana Noel 1978

ISBN 0 00 211370 8

Set in Pilgrim
Made and Printed in Great Britain by
William Collins Sons & Co Ltd Glasgow

For the 'Nan' of this story
In most loving memory and gratitude

PART ONE

I was five and a fidget. Occasionally I had a twitch, too, because if I saw anyone making odd faces or blinking a lot like Great-Uncle Joe I had to try it myself, over and over again, to see what it felt like. Nobody in the big Victorian house where I lived with Grannie, Grandpapa and Aunt Clare could understand this – not even Nan who looked after me and understood everything else I did. The real trouble started when Nan and I saw a man having a fit in the Park and I was so afraid it might happen to me that I had to put my tongue out every few minutes to make sure I could pull it back in again. He couldn't.

This new twitch upset people because they thought I was being rude, so Aunt Clare told Grannie that she would deal with it. Normally she ignored me or referred to me as 'the brat', but now we went into the dining-room and, while I perched on a slippery leather chair, Aunt Clare strode up and down using such a deep, throbby voice I thought she was going to cry. No *nice* little girl could be so rude, she told me; why wasn't I sweet and grateful? In that hard year of 1920 many children went hungry in orphanages, while I had a lovely home and fourteen Great-Aunts and -Uncles. Every week-day I was given nourishing fish, cabbage, rice pudding and prunes for lunch, and a delicious slice of roast beef followed by pink jelly on Sundays.

I knew it was going to happen but I couldn't help it. Very, very quickly my tongue popped out and in – just to make sure.

'You nasty little beast!' Aunt Clare's voice wasn't throbbing any more. Seizing my shoulder, she marched me into the hall. 'Go to the Nursery at once! You'll hear more about this later!'

Unfortunately it was a Friday, and while Grannie was a lovely, forgiving sort of person, her sisters were not, and at least four of them came to tea with her regularly on Friday afternoons, and Aunt Clare was usually there too, so I knew she would tell them. Things weren't helped by Nan and me meeting Great-Aunt Gussie outside the drawing-room door on our long climb up to the sixth-floor Nursery, carrying our daily penny coconut pyramids in a bag for tea.

Great-Aunt Gussie had a square, red face, short white hair, wore hot tweed suits and carried an ebony cane.

'Ha! What have you got there, Diana?' she boomed in a bass voice, screwing in her monocle and looking down at me with dislike.

'It's none of your business,' I answered very politely, imitating Great-Aunt Alicia who once said that to me. Besides our coconut pyramids *were* private.

'Really, child!' Great-Aunt Gussie marched into the drawing-room, slamming the door behind her.

'Oh, darling,' Nan said anxiously as we stopped on the fourth floor to light the gas ring under our kettle in the bathroom. 'That wasn't very polite. She's sure to complain to Grannie.' We set off up the final two flights of stairs, the carpet changing from brown-patterned Wilton to serviceable mustard cord under our feet.

'Then *I'll* complain about her to Mother!' I said loudly, with no conviction at all. We both knew that Mother was an empty threat – merely a slightly quicker form of whistling in the dark when things looked bad. She was Grannie and Grandpapa's elder daughter and visited us in London twice a year for a weekend, and it never occurred to me that we were closely related. Her forbiddingly glamorous figure always smelt so gorgeous that once I was nearly sick when she bent down to peck my cheek on her arrival. Until she said goodbye three days later, Nan and I scarcely saw Mother during these visits; she spent all her time going out or else laughing and whispering with Aunt Clare in the

'Clumsy as ever!' snorted Great-Aunt Gussie, but Grannie's hand was protectingly round my shoulder and she said: 'It's not really clumsiness, my dear, she's just all arms and legs, aren't you, Diana?' and she smiled, until she guiltily remembered that her sisters were waiting for That Child To Be Disciplined, Elizabeth – You're Spoiling Her. Grannie sighed so softly that only I heard it.

'I'm distressed to hear that you were very rude to Great-Aunt Gussie this afternoon.' She looked at me with reproachful brown eyes. 'And, you know, you've already upset Aunt Clare and a lot of other people with that nasty habit of putting your tongue out at them . . .' Her voice trailed off, defeated by the disapproving silence all round us. Aunt Clare wasn't there, but that wasn't going to help. I knew that Great-Aunt Gussie believed in a good thrashing, while Great-Aunt Alicia once shut my cousin Peter in the linen cupboard for a whole afternoon for being rude; Great-Aunt Fidge's ideas on punishment were unknown but Nan and I had just read Ali-Baba and I was terrified she might suggest boiling oil.

The flickery pain over my eye was getting worse and the churning had got up to the bottom of my chest. I wanted desperately to explain to Grannie about Nan's and my coconut pyramids being private and the man in the Park having a fit. I opened my mouth, not knowing if any words would come – and just had time to turn my head before being sick into the fender. Grannie stroked my hair while reaching over to ring the bell with her other hand. Great-Aunt Fidge waved a lace handkerchief that smelt of mothballs in front of her face and started moaning, while Great-Aunt Gussie stamped to the door and thundered up the stairs for Nan.

Grandpapa always walked to and from his office across the Park in a tall, black silk hat and morning coat. When he came in that evening he sent for Nan, said it was a pity that I seemed to have upset everybody, and I was to have no cake, jam or sweets for a week.

So removed was our Nursery world up on the sixth floor

that neither he nor Grannie realized that this would be no punishment at all. My sick-attacks often lasted four days and after that Nan made me stay in bed two more days 'for safety' and fed me entirely on arrowroot and barley water. Only Cook and the three maids had any inkling of what Nan and I were doing as they toiled past us going up the final, seventh flight of stairs to bare, white rooms where they slept on black iron bedsteads. It wasn't considered 'right' for them actually to call in on us – Nan got all her chatting done when she joined them in the basement kitchen for supper – but when I was ill Cook sometimes put her head round the door to hand in a kindly Thermos of Bovril for the night or Charlesworth, our elderly parlourmaid, wheezed 'Good-night, Miss', as she passed. No wonder she was wheezing by the time she got to us; every night she put Grannie's heavy silver tea-set into a baize bag and hauled it up to hide under her bed in case of burglars. A few months later when Aunt Clare, who specialized in brief crazes, acquired an odd-shaped Pekinese puppy which she quickly tired of, Charlesworth took him up to bed with her too, under the other arm. She never used his smart name, Ming, but called him 'Petty' and fed him chocolates until he was as wheezy as she was. I think they were happy.

Every afternoon Nan and I went for a walk in Kensington Gardens. The walk really consisted of getting there and back because, as soon as we'd said 'Good afternoon' to the Balloon Woman who sat at the gate in a black poke-bonnet and shawl, and ignored the Windmill Man (Nan said he didn't smell nice and Celluloid windmills might easily catch on fire), there was Nanny Warriss waiting for us on the very first seat inside. Nanny Warriss was Nan's great friend. They always went out together on their afternoons off, looking at the shops in Oxford Street before catching a bus to see Nanny Warriss's cousin Mary who wasn't quite all there but gave them Abernethy biscuits for tea and had six canaries.

Nanny Warriss looked after two little girls called Huberta and Deborah Watson-Leigh. Apart from their beautiful names, I admired them so fervently that I never managed to play with them very well. They wore black, furry tricorne hats and navy-blue coats with gold buttons in winter, while in summer they had flowery Liberty prints and pale gold straw hats wreathed with flowers. Aunt Clare always came with Nan and me to buy my clothes, and her choice never varied: at Daniel Neal she demanded one navy serge skirt on a cream bodice and white flannel shirt-blouses for winter, and two white serge skirts with plain cotton blouses for summer. On top went a navy gaberdine coat – two inches too big to allow for growing – a hard, black felt hat with a circular brim and a cream panama for sunny weather.

The panama caused even more trouble one summer than my spasmodic twitches; it had a most fascinating and extraordinary smell which I obviously couldn't enjoy while it was on my head, so I began taking it to bed with me during my afternoon rest, sniffing away at it while turning the pages of a picture book. Nan got so worried that she finally mentioned it to Grannie, who told our family doctor. Poor man, he didn't know quite what to do – I learnt long afterwards that people who keep sniffing at hot-waterbottles and mackintoshes are usually mad, but panama hats were an unknown quantity.

Dr McLain was a rosy little Scotsman. Because Grannie was delicate and I usually had something, he visited our house quite a lot. When he came in the mornings he was very brisk and prescribed more grey powders for me and beef tea for Grannie. But if he couldn't come until the afternoon, his words slipped about a bit and he smelt like the decanters on the dining-room sideboard. On these occasions he forgot the grey powders, tickled me under the chin and said that if a cat could look at a king why shouldn't I sniff at my hat?

The day that I first met my father, Dr McLain had to be sent for in the middle of the night. Our Nursery was very small, with the two beds along one wall, reaching from the windowsill to the door; then we had a big round table by the window, covered with a red plush cloth, a tall white cupboard full of shelves, a little fireplace with a high guard, a rocking-chair, a chintz curtain hiding the pegs where we hung our outdoor clothes, and a marble-topped washstand with a daisy-patterned jug and basin. On the tiny patch of lino left in the middle of the room was a faded yellow mat with wavy blue lines surrounding a single, brown rose. And recently we had acquired a magic screen which was wedged round the top of my bed. This was made of dark-red silk panels and had three blue birds, embroidered in silk, flying across the top; when the light was out and the fire flickering these birds really *did* fly – their wings moved and the tufty feathers on their heads blew up and down. The screen was another offering from Great-Uncle Patrick in Hong-Kong, but Grandpapa got angry whenever he saw it. Apparently Great-Uncle Patrick had forgotten to pay freight on it, so when it was delivered Grandpapa had to pay out a lot of money before the Railway man would bring the crate in. When Grannie laughed (Great-Uncle Patrick was her favourite brother), he stared at her over the top of his spectacles and said he never wanted to see the blasted thing again; so Grannie had it sent up to us.

On the night my father arrived back after a Very Distinguished War followed by a long-drawn-out secret mission to the Far East, Nan was knitting in the firelight and I was in bed with my eyes half shut so as to see my flying birds better.

Suddenly we heard voices and laughter coming up the stairs. Nan bustled out to say 'Ssh', but came back smiling and switched on our bright centre light under its white china shade.

All at once the Nursery was full of this enormous person. I think Aunt Clare was behind him but I never saw her. As he walked towards my bed his head bumped against the light and, looking up, all I could see was his black moustache jumping about above a big, laughing mouth.

'Diana, *what* a lovely surprise!' said Nan. 'This is your Daddy, darling.'

I had always thought 'Daddy' was just the name of a

rather remote man in uniform in a silver frame who stood on the drawing-room piano. Now, Nan's voice sounded as if he was something special to do with me. Before I could sort this out he bent down and scooped me out of bed, tossing me up so that my head missed the ceiling by half an inch and my supper junket went plap-plap in my tummy. His face was red and shiny as I flew past it, and he kept on laughing. Then he put me down on the bed and pulled something out of his pocket.

'Look, Diana. I've brought this for you all the way from Japan.'

He couldn't know that I'd had a horror of dolls ever since Great-Aunt Fidge whispered to me that they were really dead babies. And the one he was holding towards me wasn't even a baby – it was a tiny dead woman with slit eyes and, when he jiggled something in her back, her stiff black hair shot up and down with a creak.

Nan was beside me. 'Take it, darling,' she said urgently, feeling, I suppose, that the meeting wasn't being a roaring success. 'It's so kind of Daddy to bring such a beautiful doll for you.'

Obediently I stuck out my hand and Daddy, grateful for some reaction, however small, from the pale whey-faced child he had fathered on a one-night honeymoon nearly six years ago, crammed the doll at me so quickly that the head fell off and a slow trickle of pink sawdust began to run out on to my eiderdown. I leapt out of bed and crouched down behind Nan screaming: 'Take her away – she's *not* dead – she's bleeding *pink* . . .'

Two hours later I was still crying, and refused to go near my bed in case parts of the doll had somehow got under the pillow. When Dr McLain came he told Nan to crush two aspirins in a spoonful of jam. 'That'll quieten her down,' he said.

It was many months before I saw my father again.

School hadn't entered my life so far because I was considered too highly strung, so, as no other children had ever played much part inside the safe chrysalis that was Nan and me, it didn't strike me that there was anything unusual about our way of living. Huberta and Deborah didn't count because, during our daily encounters in the Park, while I never got tired of looking at their shining curls and smart clothes, so they never tired of trying to push me over or throw balls at me. They nick-named me 'Wonky' and conversation was very limited.

Grannie, being so delicate, took life very easily and, secretly, she felt that I was fully educated already. She herself taught me to read from a thick book with tiny print called *Bobby and Belle*. Bobby and Belle were outlined in gilt on the cover, and were both very fat with ringlets and sailor collars, and all their adventures had very dull, moral endings. Still, by the time we got to page 260 I could read perfectly. Later, I used to spend an hour in Grannie's bedroom every morning while she was having her hair done, reading aloud all the Psalms for that day and then a few pages in either French or Italian; that I couldn't understand a single word didn't worry her at all – she spoke four languages fluently herself and said the important thing was for me to acquire a faultless accent. I never managed to achieve one, but she thought I had, which came to the same thing.

However, school was, in fact, almost upon me – although the day when the decision was finally made started as ordinarily as any other.

It was a Saturday and, as usual, the whole household gathered in the dining-room punctually at ten to eight while Grandpapa read family prayers. Grannie, Aunt Clare and I sat along the wall by the fireplace while Cook, Nan and the maids sat on a row of harder chairs in front of the bookcase opposite. It was rude to stare, so we all looked piously up at the ceiling or out of the window while Grandpapa read the lesson at the head of the dining-room table between us. Only Nan and I sometimes looked at each other in a friendly way because, if our kettle had been slow in boiling for her early tea and my tapes and buttons had given us trouble, we both knew that she still had her nightie on under her long, grey cotton dress and white apron.

When Grandpapa knelt down, shutting his eyes and propping the big prayer book against Grannie's porridge plate, we all turned our backs on one another and knelt against our chairs. I was busy unpicking a piece of leather trimming along the side of mine, but that day I suddenly realized I'd been given a different chair! The trimming was stuck firmly in position. I was so surprised that I forgot to join in 'Our Father' when the time came, and Grandpapa stopped after 'Thy will be done' and said:

'Diana! We shall start again from the beginning.'

Afterwards, while I was waiting in the hall for Nan to bring our breakfast tray up from the kitchen, Charlesworth hobbled towards me; her feet bothered her dreadfully and she spent all her afternoons off queueing in the panel doctor's surgery to see if he could help them.

'Miss Diana,' she said severely, 'don't you let me catch you monkeying with the leather on my chairs ever again! Lucky I caught you at it before more damage was done!' Then she paused to control her bunions before marching bravely and without a wince into the dining-room with the Wedgwood porridge bowl and a silver jug of cream.

'Do all the dining-room chairs belong to Charlesworth?' I asked Nan as we panted upstairs behind our own rapidly cooling porridge and boiled eggs.

'No, darling, but she does the polishing so she's proud of them,' Nan explained, breathing heavily up the home stretch.

Saturday mornings were usually lovely. Nan and I went to the Grocer to cash the weekly housekeeping cheque for Grannie. It was the only big shop near us, and to me it was paradise. The floor was covered with clean, soft sawdust and all the most delicious smells in the world came to meet us as we went in through the glass doors. While Nan was doing the cheque with the cashier-lady who sat in a high glass box in the middle, sending little wooden pepper-pots full of change back to any assistant who had taken money from a customer – she actually spun them back along high wires – I walked alone along the counters. Nan didn't take very long so I had to plan in advance which things I wanted to look at most – but Bacon and Ham nearly always won. A specially bright light hung low over the neat piles of rashers on their marble slab, and at least two York hams were decorated all over with flower patterns in parsley. A young man in a stiff white coat often sharpened his shining silver knife while I watched. Somehow I never connected such beauty with fried bacon or ham sandwiches at all.

But on this particular Saturday we couldn't go. The unthinkable happened and, after breakfast, Nan felt very ill. When Grannie called me downstairs and said Dr McLain was coming immediately, my world fell to pieces round me. I knew she must be going to die. In fact my premature grief was so impossible to bear that I locked myself in the lavatory (absolutely forbidden) and gave myself up to the tragic vision of myself in dead black from head to foot, with a widow's veil and black kid gloves as well, standing, the only mourner, by a grave piled high with flowers.

Nan's funeral was my only reality, so when first Charlesworth and then Aunt Clare knocked on the door commanding me to open it and come out, my heartbroken, bereft sobs were absolutely genuine. Later I vaguely heard a confused murmur of voices outside, with phrases like 'the fire brigade' and 'Jones the Square gardener has a ladder', but they didn't register at all. But Nan did. Suddenly, beautifully, her voice came gently through the door.

'Diana, it's me, Nan. Open the door, darling, I'm feeling ever so much better now.'

Grave and flowers melted away. I fumbled frantically with the stiff brass bolt and flew straight out into her arms. She was in her dressing-gown with her hair in two plaits over her shoulders – but she was alive and smiling. Still, Dr McLain said she must stay in bed and keep quiet as he thought she was getting influenza, so nobody seemed to know what to do with me. Then Nan remembered that this was the day when Mrs Cooley, our sewing woman, came; perhaps I could spend the morning with her in the linen room, have lunch in the dining-room just this once, and then Maisie, the housemaid, would take me for a walk.

Mrs Cooley was so timid that she always put big felt

slippers on over her shoes when she arrived, so that she could creep silently up to the linen room next to our Nursery without even disturbing a fly. There she sat in a corner, mending sheets and pillow cases, until Cook blew on the Speaking Tube that we had in every room, to tell her kitchen lunch was ready. Mrs Cooley reminded me of the Flopsy Bunnies, she was so tiny and round, with little bright eyes and a nose that twitched gently while she sewed.

But until this morning I never knew about her teeth. She wasn't expecting me, so they were the first thing I noticed, a gleaming white smile sitting beside her on a blue saucer. As soon as she saw me she dropped her needle and quickly popped them back in, but I was so excited I forgot to say 'Good Morning' in my hurry to beg her to take them out again.

'Oh no, Miss Diana,' she protested in her whispery voice. 'What would your Grandma say?'

I couldn't see that it had anything to do with Grannie at all, and said so. I'd never known – and probably Grannie didn't, either – that such things as false teeth existed, and they seemed the most wonderful invention in the world. My teeth were horrid, and Nan had to take me to Mr Bull the dentist at least four times a year. He smelt of peppermint balls and, telling dreadful lies about how little it would hurt, proceeded to hold my mouth open with one large hand and push the drill in with the other; the grinding would go on and on until I was a clenched ball of misery in his high green chair. Now if I had teeth that lived on a saucer, Nan could take those to Mr Bull instead and he would never have to hurt me again.

I explained this eagerly to Mrs Cooley, but she shook her head and her nose twitched wistfully. 'They're chronic,' she whispered. 'Pain me gums something shocking and if I get a hard bit of meat with me dinner they're liable to jump right out on the plate. Mister Cooley, now, 'e don't fancy 'is own bit of dinner after that.'

I quite saw that it could be awkward having teeth that jumped out at people, but somewhere here I felt there was a useful idea if only I could find it. I climbed up on to the old rocking-horse that lived in the linen room because he was too big for the Nursery, and creaked slowly to and fro while I tried to think.

When she thought I wasn't looking, Mrs Cooley slipped the beautiful teeth out and wrapped them in her handkerchief. Talking was impossible after that because her lips went into little pleats and folded themselves in, so I borrowed her scissors, found some cardboard to cut, and we spent the rest of the morning in busy, companionable silence.

Aunt Clare was Grannie's younger daughter. She was tall and smart with a roman nose that went pink out of doors and big brown eyes. Grannie and Grandpapa were very proud of her and used to introduce her as 'Our youngest, unmarried daughter', in the sort of tone that implied she could have married the Prince of Wales, of course, only she was in no hurry to make up her mind. But they had stopped doing that the summer before, as Nan finally explained after I pestered her: 'Your poor aunt has been Crossed in Love.'

I wanted far more than this bald statement, so Nan got out the toasting-fork and we crouched over the Nursery fire burning our first two bits of bread to a cinder while she told me.

Apparently, when we were all having our 'abroad' holiday the year before, a Frenchman – a Count, no less – had twice asked Aunt Clare to dance with him in the hotel after dinner and once he'd carried her towel up from the beach after bathing. Then, without even saying goodbye, he vanished one evening while Aunt Clare was waiting hopefully for him in the hotel conservatory, wearing her new gold dress that she hadn't put on before because the armholes were too tight. All day, Nan said, he had been going on to Grannie about how much he loved flowers and giving Aunt Clare very French looks while he was talking, so of course she took the hint and felt sure he was inviting her to join him in the conservatory later on so that he could Speak.

I sighed in ecstasy and urged Nan to go on. Although she

and I went abroad every year with the rest of the family, we never saw anyone much in the big hotels we stayed at. In fact the only difference it made to us was that we never slept very well at first because Nan said foreigners were thieves and robbers, so she made us both keep all our valuables under our pillows. This meant, under mine: our purses (because I got threepence a week), the box with my christening brooch and bracelet in it which I wore for supper, and my bible; Nan hadn't room for these under her pillow because she persuaded Grannie to let her sleep on her flat leather jewel case, as well as on our passports and the picture of Nan's baby sister in a silver locket who died when she was two.

For the rest, our normal Nursery life went on as usual. Grandpapa always took a small sitting-room for us in the hotel where our breakfast and lunch were served, while the others went down to the big dining-room. In the evenings Nan and I put on our best clothes and went down there, too – but an hour before anyone else so that we sat among hundreds of empty tables all on our own. We never ate much at these suppers because usually about ten waiters looked after us, having nothing else to do, and they chattered away in what Nan called 'their heathen tongue' and smiled and bowed a lot, so that it seemed rude to sit chewing and swallowing as if they weren't there at all.

So now I had to try and imagine Aunt Clare's French Count, as I had never seen anyone like him myself. Willowy, I decided, a beautiful, sad man with a long moustache who wrote poetry and maybe even carved his heart on a tree like a young man I had once watched in the Park.

'What happened then? After he'd vanished?' I prompted Nan as she went on burning toast and not saying anything.

'Nothing, I believe,' she said. 'At least, not that your Grandmother ever mentioned.' Nan used to do Grannie's hair for her when we were on holiday, so they talked to each other quite a lot then.

I felt horribly let down.

'Your Aunt Clare took it very much to heart,' Nan went on, breaking off the burnt crusts and putting margarine on the bits that were only just dark brown. 'She wore black every evening after that until we came home, and never went near the ballroom. So Grannie doesn't say anything about her not being married now.'

I was half in love with my own vivid picture of the dreamy, poetic Count by then, and privately I didn't think much of Aunt Clare's behaviour. If the armholes were tight she might have had to change her dress first, but then surely she should have gone out to look for him? Suppose he'd been run over? Or bound, gagged and robbed like the hero of a serial I was reading in *Little Folks*?

I still worried about him now and then when everything was quiet and, working silently beside Mrs Cooley, it suddenly occurred to me that he might have been struck down by the plague. But I didn't have time to ask Mrs Cooley if she knew exactly what the plague was like, because Maisie called me to come and brush my hair and wash my hands properly before lunch. She told me that Grannie and Grandpapa had gone out so I should be having lunch alone with Aunt Clare and the new Curate from St Paul's, so I was to be sure and eat up nicely and behave myself.

I nodded but said nothing. I had the most lovely surprise for Aunt Clare and the Curate, though I'd really meant it for Grannie. Still, they'd be so pleased with me I might even be allowed to leave my rice pudding and prunes.

When I went into the drawing-room they were standing by the fireplace drinking glasses of sherry. Aunt Clare was being very jolly and modern, twirling her long jade beads and laughing at whatever the Curate said.

'Hello, Scrap,' she said, just as if we hugged and kissed every day and shared jokes. 'Come and say how do you do to Mr Pender.'

I held out my hand, looking up at them both so that they could share the glorious benefit of my smile. But my beautiful cardboard teeth fell out on to the carpet.

'Diana!' It was obvious that we'd never shared any jokes now. Aunt Clare bent down and, with infinite disgust, she picked up my morning's careful work made from the shiny white lid of a shoebox, but yellowing a little from getting damp inside my mouth, and threw it straight into the fire.

'Better make them from orange peel next time,' Mr Pender said in a warm, smiley sort of voice. 'They last better.'

'It was an extremely rude thing to do when she knew you were here.' Aunt Clare tried not to sound as cross as she felt.

'I'm sure you didn't do it to be rude, did you, Diana?'

My eyes hurt terribly with keeping them wide open so that the tears would dry up instead of spilling out, but I took a quick look at Mr Pender. He was smiling and he had a lovely face, all brown and bumpy with one eye higher up than the other; his teeth looked very like Mrs Cooley's and I hoped they were and that they'd jump out at lunch and put Aunt Clare off her bit of dinner.

'I wasn't being rude,' I managed over the wobble in my throat. 'My teeth are rather ugly and I thought white cardboard ones would look nicer.'

He laughed and patted my head, but I knew Aunt Clare thought I was being impertinent. Luckily, before she could say any more the gong went and we all walked down to the dining-room.

It was exciting being in the dining-room during the day because even if the sun was shining outside it felt like bed-time without actually having to go to bed. The walls were very, very dark red and there were long red plush curtains with bobbles on; thick, cream lace curtains patterned all over with roses covered the whole big window so that, while nobody could see in, only a very little yellowy light could get in either. The furniture was heavy and dark, too, and the enormous table, covered with a white cloth, looked cold and lonely when it was only laid for three people.

Charlesworth smiled and put a flat cushion on the leather chair for me; I wanted to ask her how she knew that leather stuck to my bare legs, and to say how kind it was of her to think of it, but I was afraid Aunt Clare wouldn't think it interesting enough for Mr Pender to hear.

They had little silvery bowls with brown jelly in front

of each of them. 'Don't worry, Miss, your lunch is coming,' Charlesworth whispered as she passed behind me to pour out some wine.

Aunt Clare was laughing again, telling Mr Pender that she would simply love to get up a concert with him to help raise funds for repairing the church roof.

Charlesworth brought a silver crested dish and handed it to Mr Pender (he had eaten his jelly very fast so Aunt Clare did, too). There was the most gorgeous smell, and for a minute I wondered if I would get a special lunch, too. But on a quick count I saw that there were only four brown cutlets with little frills on, two curly patterns of mashed potato and two heaps of green peas.

Then it was my turn. My hotplate had a silver cover on because this was the dining-room, and Charlesworth took it off as if there might be a surprise underneath after all; but there was my piece of white fish in a puddle of milk, the sieved floury potato done with no butter because of me being sick such a lot, and the cabbage.

I had managed two mouthfuls, and Aunt Clare was just suggesting which songs she might sing herself at the concert, when the sad loss of my precious cardboard teeth, now burnt to ashes upstairs, came home to me. My mouth was full and I drew a deep breath to stop from crying – but I breathed in some cabbage as well, and choked so badly that little specks of green flew all over the stiff white cloth and both Aunt Clare and Mr Pender had to thump me on the back, telling each other that it would be all right as long as I didn't turn blue.

After that Aunt Clare rang the bell and asked Charlesworth to remove me and my lunch to Grandpapa's study next door.

The study was small, darker even than the dining-room, and special. In spite of Grandpapa's pipe rack and a few ink splodges on his open blotter on the desk, it felt as if nobody alive had spent a single minute in it, ever, since time began. A queer, peaceful dankness pervaded everything, from the faded leather-bound books in two mahogany bookcases to the ancient parrot who dozed in a large cage

24

in front of the fireplace where no fire ever burned. A wing-chair in worn brown leather, a photograph of Great-Grand-father glaring out indignantly above an enormous white beard, and the small table on which I was to eat, completed the furnishing.

The table fascinated me. It was a slab of pink, mottled marble on four black legs with a shelf halfway down so that you had to sit sideways. If you looked at the top quickly, it was like the German sausage Grannie always ordered for the Choir Supper. But when I half shut my eyes, like I did with our screen in the Nursery, the mottled lines split the pink surface into faces. I had already found a witch, a dog with its tongue out, and Great-Aunt Gussie, when Charlesworth came back to see how I was getting on.

I wasn't. My fish lay cold and gluey and the cabbage was yellowing round the edges.

'Now come on, Miss Diana. Cook says your rice pudding will dry up if she has to keep it warm much longer.'

I simply couldn't. If my rice pudding turned into brown rock I couldn't possibly eat what was on the plate in front of me. Up in the Nursery Nan and I had a system : for every four mouthfuls of fish I ate she would give me a taste of her rabbit or stew on a fork. Then, when her own lunch was finished, she read aloud, always something very exciting so that fish and cabbage were swallowed in sheer amaze-ment at whatever adventure we were rapt in.

When Charlesworth grumbled off I looked helplessly round the study until my eye lighted on the parrot. I used to think he was stuffed because he sat, day after day, with his eyes shut and his feathers unruffled, but Nan said it was just as well he slept so much because, in the very early morning, he made lots of noise and, as Great-Uncle Joe had bought him from a sailor, all he could do was swear.

Carrying my plate very carefully, I approached the tall cage. The closed, leathery eyelids never moved. Between the bars there was a handy little gap just above his seed pot, and another over the water jar.

'Poor Polly,' I said softly. 'You must be as tired of dull old seed as I am of fish and cabbage.' He didn't move, so I balanced some cabbage on a fork and pushed it through on to his food. It made the cage look more friendly, so I put in some more. I was so anxious not to drop any on the floor and leave traces that I forgot Polly himself altogether. Suddenly he moved, stretching his neck and spreading his wings out and back again. I dropped my plate, face down, on the carpet; but seeing him move was far more important. He started to squawk and it didn't make sense at all – until he began to talk.

A few moments later Aunt Clare put her head round the door.

'All right, Diana?' she asked, so pleasantly that I knew Mr Pender must be just behind her. 'Mr Pender and I are going up to the drawing-room for coffee now.'

'Bugger the bastard,' I replied conversationally.

That evening Aunt Clare spent an hour with Grannie and Grandpapa telling them that I was not only rude, disobedient and a thorough nuisance, but was now swearing like a trooper and must go to school even if it made me be sick every day for a week.

Grannie called me into her bedroom while she was changing into the silvery, soft velvet tea-gown that she always wore for dinner at home. I loved it when her jewel case was open and I could look at her treasures. The longest pearl necklace came halfway down my serge skirt and, when I'd balanced her diamond star brooch on my hair, I used to put on her big, shiny rings, keeping my fingers tight together afterwards so that they wouldn't fall off while I watched them glinting and flashing in the mirror.

'Diana, darling.' Grannie never looked at me when there was something difficult to say, and I loved her extra much for this because I wouldn't have known how to look back without getting my eye-blinking twitch through staying so solemn.

Now she looked very hard at the little chintz chest-of-drawers that stood by the dressing-table and held all her Brussels lace collars.

'Diana,' she started again. 'Would you like to go to school?'

I was so surprised that I put my tongue out and back twice without knowing I was doing it.

'Don't do that, darling,' Grannie countered automatically; and went on: 'Most little girls of your age go, I believe, and you might enjoy it.'

'I'll hate it,' I said passionately. It was the most frightening thing I could possibly imagine – no more Nan or games of Snap or hot milk with two drops of peppermint in it on cold mornings. Just me, alone, with lots of children like Huberta and Deborah laughing and calling me 'Wonky'. Frantic with terror, I burst into tears and buried my head in her lap.

'Oh, no – please, please no.' The sobs were exploding from somewhere so deep inside me that each word came out in two pieces with a hiccupping gulp in the middle.

Grannie was upset.

'Oh, darling. Don't cry like that,' she entreated, putting her arms round me and gathering me up on to her lap. 'All children go to school sooner or later, you know, and I'm sure you'll be happy.' She stroked the hair gently back off my hot, splotchy forehead. 'You'd only be going for the mornings to start with. Why, you'll hardly know that Nan has left you there before she'll be back to fetch you home again.'

The gulping and hiccupping wouldn't stop.

'Besides, you'll make lots of little friends,' Grannie went on soothingly, her kind brown eyes glancing over my damp hair and crumpled blouse but never looking directly at my hideously swollen eyes. 'You ought to have children of your own age to play with.' She seemed to be talking more to herself than to me. 'I know how happy you are with Nan, but there are lovely games that can only be played among children . . . and you'll learn a lot, Diana, because you're a clever girl.' She smiled straight down at me. 'Too clever, sometimes, I believe!'

*

27

Next day Nan told me that Grannie had ordered the car and gone off to interview the headmistress of the school that Huberta and Deborah went to. The news that they would definitely be some of the 'other children' Grannie had pictured so vividly yesterday evening threatened to bring on another storm of weeping, but Nan went on quickly :

'Nanny Warriss says they're ever so happy there. The youngest class has twenty really nice girls in it, she says – in fact one of them is actually the daughter of a Princess!' Nan and I looked at each other in awe. The only princesses we knew about were fairies, though I didn't fancy being one myself after reading Cinderella and finding that, through some careless bit of magic, all my jewels and even my clothes might vanish at midnight.

'You'll like it, darling,' Nan insisted seriously. 'And I've thought of a good idea : when you've been there a while and settled down, I'll ask Grannie if we can give a little party for you, maybe for your birthday. I'm sure she'd let us use the drawing-room just for one afternoon.'

A party! I'd never been to one, and for a breathless instant I saw our drawing-room lined with footmen in powdered wigs while my guests and I, become miraculously tall and grown-up, swirled round in crinolines, satin coats and buckled shoes, while towering iced cakes and jellies on silver dishes awaited our pleasure in the dining-room below.

'Oh Nan!' I breathed out again, and accepted that it would be me in my white serge skirt and Assorted Iced Fancies from the ABC like Nan sometimes had to buy for drawing-room tea if Cook was too rushed off her feet to bake. Still, a *party* . . .

The Speaking Tube in the Nursery made its hissing sound; all the others in the house whistled, but ours hadn't since I dropped my toy thimble into it to see if it would go right down and fall out in the kitchen. It was Grannie wanting to see Nan at once.

Nan and I were busy winding wool round the back of a chair ready for her to start knitting a warm scarf for the winter, so while she was gone I was able to play my favourite game. As I wound the wool, neatly and very fast, I was Jenny, the most beautiful girl in a big factory. Jenny had been stolen away from her father's palace as a baby while her wicked uncle put his ugly daughter in her place so that she should inherit all the jewels and grow up to marry a prince. Jenny was left on a cottage doorstep, but in spite of her poor clothes everybody loved her. She had big blue eyes and long, curly golden hair that never needed washing because it shone so brightly. Her foster-parents were terribly poor, so when Jenny was seventeen she had to go to work in the factory.

There she stood in bitterly cold weather in her ragged dress and bare feet, her gold hair shining like fire in the single ray of light that came in through a high, slitty window, her slim white hands weaving the coloured wools in and out, making beautiful patterns ten times more quickly than anyone else there. Sometimes Jenny was making carpets and sometimes just great patterns that were so lovely they made me want to cry because I couldn't even describe them properly in my mind. But I never did cry because the patterns were working up to the most exciting part of the whole story, the moment when the factory door crashed open and there, with a snowstorm raging behind him, stood the young owner, Mr Anstruther. He wore sponge-bag trousers, white spats, a long black cloak with a fur collar and a tall silk hat like Grandpapa's. He was the handsomest man in the whole world.

Pausing, he saw the light falling on Jenny's golden hair, and in a flash he was at her side. His strong, brown hands gently released her soft ones from their dreadful toil and, clasping her into his cloak, he said: 'You are the most beautiful girl of my wildest dreams. From now on you shall have chicken and macaroons to eat every day of your life!' And they lived happily ever after.

Sometimes Mr Anstruther promised Jenny birthday cake instead, only it was usually macaroons because Grannie had a box of twelve big, flat brown ones with almonds on top delivered from Buzzard's every Saturday morning; but Aunt Clare told everybody they were unwholesome for children and I wouldn't be allowed to taste one until I was twelve.

The factory door had just crashed open when Nan came hurrying back, looking pink and flustered.

'I've got to go down and help Charlesworth with the spare room,' she said. 'A telegram's come to say your Great-Aunt Primrose is coming to stay the night and it's Maisie's day off.'

'Which is Great-Aunt Primrose and did Grannie see the school?' I wanted to know, hating to stop the game before Jenny got all her lovely rewards.

'Yes, yes.' Nan was struggling into her working apron. 'Grannie will tell you all about it herself when you go down after tea. You'll start in September. Now come along, you can lend us a hand if you like – better than staying up here on your own.'

I gabbled Jenny's happy ending under my breath and then asked Nan again: 'Have I ever seen Great-Aunt Primrose?'

'No. She's Grandpapa's sister and she never leaves her house in Portsmouth as a rule. Her husband died and left her a fortune, I believe,' added Nan who, like me, loved happy endings if there were any going.

The spare room was hardly ever used except when Mother came, and it had a heavy, spooky feeling with all the dust sheets over the mahogany furniture. '. . . Not but what you weren't born in here,' said Charlesworth over her shoulder while I was polishing the wardrobe mirror. I stared at my reflection and felt crawly all over. How horrible of Mother to find me in this ghosty, dark place when she could have gone to a sunny garden filled with flowers, like the one round the cottage where Nan and I stayed at Easter after I'd had mumps.

'You feeling all right, Diana?' asked Nan, crackling open big, embroidered linen sheets for the bed. 'You're not getting one of your heads now, are you? She looks peaky,' she added to Charlesworth in a worried voice.

'I think I am,' I said, more because I didn't want to stay in the room than anything else. All the same, by the time I reached the Nursery it had become true. The familiar flickering began and I pressed a hand against the right side of my head, too sad at the thought of a tiny, new baby waiting all alone to be found by Mother in that awful room to have any heart for Jenny and Mr Anstruther in the factory.

Instead, I thought a lot about finding babies. Grannie had told me long ago that that's how it was done, but it seemed a very haphazard arrangement. How did you know when to go and where? And what happened if you found one that was meant for someone else? I decided to ask Grannie much more about it – but I began to understand why I'd been left in the spare room: it was so handy. Since Mother obviously didn't like children, she probably wouldn't have bothered to go all the way to a country garden.

This made me feel better, and when Nan came up I asked if she thought Great-Aunt Primrose would arrive in a big car or even a carriage as she was very old as well as being very rich.

Nan didn't know. Nobody knew what to expect until Charlesworth answered the front door at half past four and found a cross old woman in rusty black who had walked two miles from the railway station carrying her own shabby suitcase.

'You've kept me standing on that step for three whole minutes,' she snapped at poor Charlesworth as she stamped past into the hall wearing a pair of heavy buttoned boots. 'I imagine my sister-in-law is waiting in the drawing-room so I'll show myself up. You can bring me four thin slices of bread and butter, and a cup of weak camomile tea. Very hot, mind!'

As soon as Great-Aunt Primrose disappeared round the bend of the stairs Charlesworth was on the Speaking Tube to Nan: There wasn't a speck of camomile tea in the house; could Nan possibly run round to the chemist and see if he'd got some?

Nan and I hurried into our hats and coats, feeling as excited at doing an emergency errand at this unusual hour as if we were being asked to fight our way through the jungle bringing supplies to a beleaguered fortress.

Mr Maloney, the chemist, showed that he was surprised to see us at such a time, too, by very slightly raising his eyebrows at Nan as we went in. Mr Maloney was the most completely royal sort of person I had ever met. His shop front was kept very smart, as a window-cleaner washed down the black and gold paint every week. Three tall glass bottles decorated the window itself, one filled with green liquid, one with red and one with the dark blue of Grannie's sapphire ring. These bottles were flanked by a chaste display of lavender soap in boxes or, towards Christmas, a tasteful arrangement of sponges and bottles of eau-de-Cologne. Inside. Mr Maloney reigned supreme.

He was very, very tall and shaped like a narrow egg; even his nose hooked majestically down towards his chin. Every day he wore a high wing-collar, a silver silk cravat with a pearl pin, grey striped trousers and a black morning-coat with very long tails at the back. His voice came from far away, sighing softly down through his nose and, whatever the problem, Mr Maloney considered it carefully, pressing the tips of his fingers together. When he found the solution he would say : 'Ah, yes!' and disappear behind the glass screen that hid all his medicines. He never showed emotion of any kind, apart from a raised eyebrow or a faintly shocked 'Dear *me*,' but his smile, though it scarcely moved a muscle of his face, was lovely.

When Nan, still flustered, had poured out our predicament of Great-Aunt Primrose and the camomile tea he *did* smile, and at once we felt safe and comforted. It was All Right, we would get our supplies back to the fortress in time.

And we did. In the shape of a neat chemist's parcel, tied with pale blue string and stamped with sealing-wax, which Mr Maloney handed soothingly to Nan almost before she had finished her story.

In the end, Great-Aunt Primrose's visit lasted not one night but four, and upset our family habits and routine to such an extent that they never, in fact, quite recovered.

On the afternoon of her arrival I went down to the drawing-room half an hour later than usual, owing to Nan's and my dash to Mr Maloney. I was longing to see Grannie and to hear all about the school, but as soon as I opened the door everything looked different.

Grannie was sitting, very straight and uncomfortable, on a small sofa between the two french windows where the Vicar usually perched when he came for charity subscriptions.

In front of the fire, on one of our straight dining-room chairs which she had had brought up, Great-Aunt Primrose was pulling a buttonhook with a chipped mother-of-pearl handle out of the deep pocket in her skirt. Breathing loudly, she bent over and unbuttoned her tall black boots, easing them off with little grunts of pleasure before placing them side by side against the fender where they gave off a most interesting smell. Then, with a final grunt, she put her feet up on Grannie's lovely brocade armchair.

'Never pamper your spine, Elizabeth,' she said severely. 'Sit up straight and live to be a hundred. Only your poor old feet deserve soft cushions at the end of a good day's walk!'

I slipped silently on to the sofa beside Grannie and her hand came over and clutched both mine while we stared, fascinated, at the poor old feet as they nestled about among Grannie's precious cushions. The coarse grey woollen socks were full of holes, and two yellowish big toes poked through at the ends. The heels had what Nan called 'potatoes', but these didn't show at first because Great-Aunt Primrose's own heels were almost as grey and rough as her socks.

Charlesworth had moved some photographs off one of the spindly tables and placed a silver salver with a plate of thin bread and butter and a cup of camomile tea beside Great-Aunt Primrose's right elbow. Now she poured the tea into her saucer and drank it with loud sucking noises. The room was so quiet and tense otherwise that I felt a tickle beginning in my throat. Clenching my teeth and tipping my head back until my throat was straight and taut, I said 'Jesus Tender Shepherd Hear Me – don't let me cough' over and over in my head.

But, as Nan always reminded me when our special prayers didn't seem to be answered, it can't have been His will because, in the silence, my cough exploded, not once but four times, from being so tightly pushed back, and the last cough deposited an embarrassing blob on one of the hands Grannie was holding. Easing it carefully out of her grasp I rubbed it furtively against the side of the sofa.

'This Georgina's child?' Great-Aunt Primrose fixed her steel spectacles on me. 'Very unhealthy. Ought to make her run five miles before breakfast every day. Nothing like it.'

Obviously Grannie's mind was miles away from school so, when Nan came to fetch me, I went thankfully upstairs. We met Charlesworth on the landing outside the Nursery, coming down from changing into her frilly evening cap and apron.

'Imagine!' she said, a lifetime's tradition about not gossiping upstairs thrown to the winds. 'She's worth quarter of a million pounds and what d'you think I unpacked from her case?'

Nan and I stood like one united question-mark.

'Pigs!' announced Charlesworth. 'An old flannel nightie full of holes and over two hundred little lead pigs like you get from a toyshop! 'Cept that they're pink and clean and hers are mostly black and chipped all over.'

That night Nan came up from her supper with eyes like saucers.

'What's happened?' I demanded, having sat up in bed ever since she left the Nursery, to make sure no thrilling revelations came along while I was asleep.

'Diana! You should've settled down long ago,' she protested – just to observe the formalities. We both ignored it.

'What's she doing now?'

'Well . . .' Since the whole household had relaxed and got cosily together over this visit, Nan sat on my bed and unpinned her apron.

'She wouldn't eat the dinner! Not one bite. And your grandmother had taken special trouble, too. It was consommé, sole and then grouse . . .' On my own strict diet of white fish, rice and prunes the richness of these delicacies passed me by, but from Nan's face I knew they must be very rare and Sunday-ish.

'No,' Nan went on, 'she told your grandfather that overeating would be the death of him and sent down for raw porridge oats and skimmed milk!'

Secretly I thought this might be an improvement on rice pudding, but in the new spirit of Us against Her that pervaded the house I gasped: 'Oh, Nan! How awful!' and really meant it.

Next morning Aunt Clare came up to the Nursery to talk to Nan. There was so much excitement in the air that even this didn't seem strange; everyone was bursting to chat with everybody else.

'She's come to London to Alter her Will,' said Aunt Clare, trying to stride dramatically up and down on our brown rose mat but giving it up when she kept bumping into the washstand. Sitting heavily in Nan's rocking-chair she pulled a packet of Gold Flake out of her cardigan pocket and lit one.

'What's a Will?' I longed to know, it was terrible to be at the heart of all this drama and then not understand an important word.

'Oh, it means how you look after your money when you're dead,' explained Aunt Clare impatiently before turning back to Nan and talking in a lower voice.

I was stunned. What they were saying no longer interested me at all. Over my bed hung a print of Holman Hunt's 'The Light of the World' and this gentle figure of Jesus, looking so wistful in his long nightie and crown of thorns, was my talisman against dying. Whenever I had a temperature and thought of myself being turned into a stiff, dead doll for someone else to play with, I clung to this picture. When I did die I would go through that door with Jesus and we'd go flying up to heaven on lots of pink clouds, and there would be angels with tall, feathery wings singing and playing harps and none of us would ever be lonely or eat anything we didn't like again.

In one sentence Aunt Clare had slashed through this vision.

If Nan and I were going to have to keep coming back to see what was happening down here to our threepenny-bit collection in the Petit Beurre biscuit tin, then there wasn't much point in going to heaven at all.

For the time being my twitches were forgotten. All my energies were gathered into a morbid terror of death, not only for myself but everyone else as well – specially Nan. I didn't even want Great-Aunt Primrose to die because, with so many pounds to look after, she'd be up and down all the time, never having a chance to rest her poor old feet on a rosy cloud for more than two minutes.

All the same, her visit caused a lot of trouble. When she called Cook's chicken fricassée 'a botched-up mess' and demanded a raw kipper for 'real nourishment', Cook cried all over the weekly household accounts book and blotched all the figures. Later Cook went upstairs and gave Grannie her notice but, Nan reported, they had a long talk in Grannie's room and Cook felt better. Then Maisie refused to do the spare room. She said the bed was full of nasty little pigs and the place smelt terrible because the old lady never had a good wash.

Worst of all – and unheard-of before – Grannie and Grandpapa had 'words' after breakfast on the third morning while Great-Aunt Primrose was out walking round Hyde Park to keep healthy. Charlesworth told Nan about it in a loud whisper as we were going through the hall, but I could hear easily.

'The poor Mistress,' Charlesworth wheezed. 'The old lady may be the Master's sister but it's our house she's upsetting something chronic. "Go tomorrow she must," the Mistress told him, in no uncertain words. 'Course, he didn't like it, but then he hasn't to put up with his sister all day long the way we do.'

At first I couldn't imagine Grannie being angry about anything, but when Nan nodded at Charlesworth and said: 'Some people are enough to try the patience of a Saint,' I loved Grannie more than ever.

After Great-Aunt Primrose left, our lives slowly returned to normal, except for a new closeness amongst us all. I heard Charlesworth telling Nan that the old skinflint hadn't left any money on the corner of her dressing-table for Maisie; but she did give something to me. Just as she was leaving, Nan and I were coming home from the Park, and she bent down and started trying to poke her bony fingers inside my left glove. I was frightened that she was going to scratch me for being so unhealthy, but instead I felt something small and cold lying in my palm.

'He'll be a good friend to you, better than people. Goodbye, Diana,' and, her old-fashioned black cape flapping round her like a maimed bird, Great-Aunt Primrose marched off down the Square, button-boots squeaking and her suitcase jigging in her hand. When I pulled off my glove I found the smallest, saddest lead pig I had ever seen. Apart from a trace of black enamel round his nose he had no paint left at all and one of his legs was missing. I made him a bed in a matchbox, wrapping him in cottonwool to keep him warm. But he got thrown away next time Maisie did the

Nursery. The matchbox didn't rattle so she thought it was empty.

It was time to get ready for our summer holiday. Grannie and Grandpapa decided that we should go to a spa in Switzerland so that both Grannie and I could Take the Cure. In addition to continual bilious attacks I'd developed twinges which Dr McLain diagnosed as rheumatism or, as they were in my knees, possibly growing-pains. A little later one began in my right shoulder-blade and this started a very comfortable habit of shrugging my shoulders right up to my ears and back again, several times running. I did it to see if the bad one was hurting and to make sure the good one wasn't, but Nan got very upset when I kept doing it during our walks. 'You really must stop it, Diana, people will think you're not quite right, going on like that!'

Grannie called Nan in one evening when she came to fetch me after my hour in the drawing-room. She said she had been thinking, now that I was nearly six, that it might be more fun for Nan and me to have all our meals in the big hotel at the same time as everyone else – if the Head Waiter could find us a quiet table for two where I wouldn't be in anybody's way. I hugged Grannie ecstatically and then my shoulders went up and down harder than ever because I was so happy.

'Perhaps our table could be behind a nice pillar?' Nan suggested, watching me anxiously.

It was also decided that I should have two shantung dresses to wear in the evenings, even though Nan and I would still have to have our supper fairly early before the really grand people were there to see us. I even forgot my obsession about dying for a whole day because Nan and I were to go alone to Liberty's to choose them!

Aunt Clare was spending nearly all her time in church at this stage, and when she heard about the shantung dresses she gave me a long, serious look and said: Wasn't I ready, yet, to go barefoot for Jesus and send all my clothes to some poor little naked Indian child if He wanted me to?

Of course I was when she put it like that, but I couldn't

help wondering why Jesus should want me to be a poor little naked English child instead. In fact, a lot of the time He'd have both of us naked because it would take my clothes weeks and weeks to go all the way to India. I put it to Nan, who only laughed and said:

'Don't take too much notice of your Aunt Clare just now, she's got her heart set on that Mr Pender, the Curate, and she's upset at having to leave him on his own while we go to Switzerland.'

Aunt Clare was right to be upset, actually, because when we came back he'd got engaged to the lady who sang all the solos in the choir and sucked acid-drops through the sermon. (When I couldn't stop shrugging my shoulders the Verger had put two chairs for Nan and me just behind the choir on Sundays, but she never turned round and offered us one!) The engagement made things difficult for Aunt Clare because, before we went away, she'd already organized the Parish Concert specially to be near Mr Pender all the time as soon as we came back. So when she heard he was going to be married, she told Grannie she thought she'd go round the world and be a heathen – but Grannie said that would be Much Too Pointed and, as Grandpapa was Church Warden, she must carry on bravely and not let the Parish down.

Whenever we travelled abroad Grannie, Grandpapa and Aunt Clare had first-class seats in one part of the train while Nan and I went second-class in the next coach. This was arranged because Grandpapa liked to get out and stretch his legs whenever the train stopped at a station, but I suffered from chronic train fever, and when I saw him doing this I worked myself into a dreadful state thinking he'd get left behind with all the tickets and we'd never see him again. The first time this happened the Boat Train hadn't even left Victoria Station and Grandpapa only got out to buy a paper, but before Nan knew what was happening I jumped out and ran after him, screaming:

'Come back, come *back*, Grandpapa! Oh, *please* come back, we need you!'

Everyone on the platform stared and began to laugh. Grandpapa was very angry and marched me back to Nan while people called out peculiar things at him like: 'Leaving 'em, were you?' and 'Trying to get off on the QT, eh?'

Grannie said: 'Oh, Diana. How could you?' and Aunt Clare, puffing furiously at her Gold Flake, announced loudly: 'The brat is more sickening than *East Lynne*.'

It was after that that Nan and I travelled separately.

The hotel in Switzerland was enormous and smelt of rotten eggs. Nan said that was because it was a Spa and it was the mud and sulphur I could smell from all the special baths to make us better which were down in the basement. Everyone we saw on the first day seemed very old, but Nan and I were so excited about going down to have our lunch in the dining-room that we made up a lovely story about a handsome young Duke and his beautiful Duchess who would suddenly get twinges and arrive here tomorrow so that we could watch them.

The Head Waiter was fat with a white, oily face. I kept my shoulders quite still, so he showed us to a little table by the window and handed Nan the menu with a flourish. Poor Nan took one look at it and her face went red; luckily the Head Waiter was called away for a minute because she said: 'Oh, Diana, whatever shall we do? It's all written in Foreign and I can't understand a word!'

But it was all right. It turned out that Grannie had already ordered what we were to have. It was still fish and rice for me, but the fish was brown and crispy and the pudding swirled up into peaks with a cherry on top.

Next day I told my lie. Grandpapa had given me a whole Swiss franc to spend and, although all the shops were exciting, the sweetshops were best of all. So Nan and I each bought a bar of milk chocolate and I couldn't resist a little box you could see through, filled with pink and mauve sugared almonds. Nan made me promise to eat them very slowly – perhaps one a day – but she thought they looked tempting, too.

We met Aunt Clare as we went into the hotel and I

showed her my wonderful almonds. They fascinated me so much that, when Nan went along to do Grannie's hair before dinner, I started to eat them. I meant to eat one and then stop . . . only I couldn't. I sat at the dressing-table and watched in the mirror, keeping my mouth a bit open. After a few sucks the colour disappeared, leaving a white, shiny coating of sugar; this got thinner until I could see the brown almond inside – then it was time to crunch it up and start all over again.

Aunt Clare came looking for Nan and saw the empty box.

'You revolting, greedy little pig.' Her voice was harsh. 'D'you mean to say you've guzzled all those sweets by yourself?'

It became a dreadful, ugly thing to have done instead of just watching the pale pink fade and the brown almond come through and I was frightened – frightened to have done it, and even more afraid that Nan and Grannie might be disgusted. My mind caught frantically at the most remote person I could think of and I jumped up, saying:

'No, I didn't, I *didn't* . . . I gave most of them to the Lift Man!'

When Nan came back I'd cried myself into an uneasy sleep in the armchair in our room. As she woke me I had a sticky-sweet taste in my mouth and for a moment I'd forgotten Aunt Clare. Nan's face quickly reminded me.

'You're to come down to Grandpapa's room,' she said, straightening my hair and getting out a clean handkerchief. 'You'd better sponge your face first, though . . . Oh, Diana, how could you *do* such a thing?'

As we went down one flight of stairs and along a wide carpeted passage, I felt very muddled. Obviously I'd done something as bad as those people in the Bible when God wouldn't look at them any more. But was it eating all the sweets or telling Aunt Clare I'd given them to the Lift Man to stop her saying horrible things?

Grandpapa was standing in the middle of his bedroom watching the door over the top of his spectacles. Grannie sat in a chair, a hand over her eyes, while Aunt Clare stared out of the window, smoking a Gold Flake. Nan shut the door behind us and went to stand beside Grannie. I was absolutely alone.

Grandpapa's voice surprised me. It didn't sound harsh like Aunt Clare's but sad and disappointed, which made me feel much worse.

'Why did you lie to Aunt Clare, Diana? It was a very, very wicked thing to do and has upset us all very much. You see, we never thought you capable of such a thing. You're such a fortunate little girl, you have everything we can possibly give you, and is this how you repay us? By deliberately telling a lie? Don't you understand that lying is one of the gravest sins of all?'

I was crying too much to hear any more, but at least Nan was beside me again, trying to dry my eyes, and Grannie had moved her hand and looked as if she'd like to put her arms round me. In the middle of a gulp I heard Grandpapa say: 'Now, if you're sure you've understood, we'll say no more about it this time.'

'Father! D'you mean to say you're not going to punish her?' Aunt Clare was so angry that her eyes glared. 'This child must be taught a lesson once and for all!' She was clenching her hands on the back of a chair and Grandpapa looked uncomfortable.

'Oh, I think Diana has learnt her lesson,' he began. Then, as Aunt Clare was obviously going to start again, he added quickly: 'But perhaps we should say no sweets for a week – eh, Nan?'

'A week! What's the good of that? She'll probably be sick that long after stuffing herself this evening!' I think we were all afraid of Aunt Clare by now. Nan had her arm round me and Grannie and Grandpapa stared at their daughter. 'This has to be something she'll remember all her life. It was not only a lie, but Diana didn't hesitate to implicate a total stranger. All the lift men were quite upset when I asked if they'd accepted expensive sweets from a child.' Aunt Clare looked round at us coldly. 'No, she must be forbidden sweets for the whole eight weeks we are here. *That* should make her realize what she's done!'

42

Of course I *was* sick and stayed in bed for nearly a week after that, but Nan thought up a secret plan: we would still go into these lovely sweetshops and buy things, but then she would put them away in her attaché case and I could have them, week by week, after we got home. So, when Grandpapa gave me my pocket-money each Saturday and Aunt Clare, smiling, reminded me: 'But not for sweets, Diana,' I didn't mind nearly so much.

The hotel doctor said I shouldn't take the baths after all, just drink the waters, and every morning I went with Grannie to a big room with a glass roof where we sat on wicker chairs and sipped warmish, green water out of tall tumblers. It tasted old and horrid but I didn't mind a bit. Most of the people there were English and they came and talked to us, saying what a shame it was to see a dear little girl Suffering Already. In fact one old gentleman joined us every day and patted my knees to see how they were feeling; when I told him about my shoulder he patted that, too, and asked if I'd like to go for a walk with him one afternoon as there were some beautiful woods not very far away. I was just going to say: Could we have tea out as well? when Grannie interrupted – quite sharply – to tell him I went out with my Nurse every day who made sure I didn't overdo things.

I was disappointed and told Nan all about it, but she just said: 'Some old gentlemen get a bit cranky, darling. Never mind, I'll ask Grannie if you and I can have tea out to-morrow in that nice café with the little stone elves and pixies in the garden.'

I couldn't see what was cranky about inviting me for a walk in the woods, but obviously no one was going to tell me.

When we got home I was unexpectedly quite glad to be going to school after all. What with Aunt Clare being Crossed in Love again, by Mr Pender, yet still having to go on with the Parish Concert, she made life wretched for everybody. She decided to hurry it all up in case she decided to go off round the world in spite of Grannie, therefore Nan must help her make the costumes she had promised to provide for the concert finale.

Our Nursery was just right for two but now, as soon as breakfast was over, Aunt Clare came up carrying yards of cheap coloured hessian which she spread all over our beds and the table. I felt it and it was very scratchy.

'Well!' she flared when I mentioned this, 'the man needn't think I'm going to buy silks and satins for his beastly singers as well as giving up all my time!' She always called poor Mr Pender 'the man' now, but she bought some very smart flags to wear herself since she was going to be Britannia and stand in the middle of the stage at the end singing 'Keep The Home Fires Burning'. I was sure she'd chosen that song purposely to make Mr Pender think about homes and how he might have found Aunt Clare by the fireside every evening – only now he'd be eating acid-drops with his choir lady instead. I felt very sad because I'd have liked Mr Pender as an uncle, but I did see that Aunt Clare might be a bit bossy and difficult to have by the fire, specially every day.

She certainly shouted a lot in the Nursery, and she said: 'My God, everyone in the world's against me!' when Nan cut out two left sides by mistake for a dress to be worn by 'Spirit of Peace'. I couldn't sew yet and there wasn't anywhere to sit, so all I could do was stand about and hand round pins.

But on the day before I was to start school Nan was firm. There was to be no dressmaking in our Nursery because we had special things to do. So we admired my new blazer and gym-slips that had been delivered from Gorringes after Nan sent them my measurements. After our walk we played Snap and then had Gentleman's Relish on toast and two chocolate biscuits each for tea.

Nan had found out all about the school from Nanny Warriss so we knew we'd got everything right, even to a currant bun in a bag for elevenses. I hated the thought of Nan going away, leaving me there alone, but she and Nanny Warriss had planned this, too, and we met her with Huberta and Deborah Watson-Leigh at the corner. I was so surprised when Deborah took my hand and asked me to be her Best Friend that I walked through the school door in a daze and forgot to say goodbye to Nan at all!

Within half an hour I was blindly, deliciously in love for the very first time. Her name was Miss Lawson. She had thick golden plaits folded round and round her head, and wore a brown velvet dress with a white lace collar and rows and rows of pink shell necklaces that came right down to her waist and clinked when she moved. She smiled all the time while she played the piano for us to warm up by doing bunny jumps round the room. Later we made Plasticine birds' nests with eggs in, and had just started to learn a song called 'The Camel's Hump is an Ugly Lump', when it was time to go and find Nan in the cloakroom. I wanted to cry because I shouldn't see Miss Lawson again until to-morrow.

In fact I didn't see her for two months. Doing bunny jumps was such fun that, while Nan was making our tea in the bathroom, I decided to demonstrate for her, forgetting that I was just at the top of our steep Nursery stairs. After bouncing twice on the way down to the bottom, my right arm was fractured in four places.

PART TWO

The days at school passed quickly. Of course there were breaks for colds, and for being sick if there was going to be Speech Day or an outing to a museum. But one occasion when I managed never to be sick was when Nan and I went to tea each week with Huberta, Deborah and Nanny Warriss in their lovely day nursery that looked out over the Park. Their house quite took our breath away at first, it was so light everywhere, and Huberta and Deborah had their own bathroom with a pink bath and silver taps. In ours the hot water came through a long rubber spout from the geyser, and there was a brown mark on the bottom of the bath shaped like a dog that moved if you swished the water.

Their nursery was blue and white with rabbits all over the tablecloth and Mabel Lucie Atwell mugs for the milk. Mrs Watson-Leigh sometimes came in to ask Nanny Warriss to fasten her pearls, or just to see that everything was all right. She was very tall and wore lots of filmy scarves – there was even one tied to her bracelet – and although she never remembered my name, she smiled at us. It was a queer smile, crooked, as if she had a pain somewhere, but Deborah didn't think she really had, though it was hard to be sure because she and Huberta never saw their mother alone, she always had so many visitors in the drawing-room.

At first Nan and I felt we ought to ask them back to tea with us but, as Nan said, it wasn't that we were ashamed of our Nursery, but having beds in it might make it too crowded for five people.

Soon it was almost Christmas and my birthday would be

soon afterwards, in January. It was going to be a very special Christmas because Great-Uncle Patrick and his wife were coming home from Hong-Kong and dear Great-Aunt Felicity would be back from India to show us all her husband, Great-Uncle Bart, for the very first time. Even Grannie was excited about meeting him because Great-Aunt Felicity had had such a romantic life: she was Grannie's youngest sister, and after all the others had married and left home, she had a dreadful row with her father. It started over a feather duster, Grannie said, only no one could remember the details after fifteen years; anyway, she ran away from home, taking her Post Office savings book and her silver christening mug. She left a note saying that she was going to join Great-Uncle Patrick in China and she'd marry the first man that asked her. It didn't take long as she tripped over Great-Uncle Bart's feet as soon as she boarded the ship. They were married by the Captain, so she never got to China but went straight to India with him instead.

Great-Aunt Felicity had been back to England several times since, but Great-Uncle Bart was always too busy. He grew tea and it seemed to need picking or planting the whole time. She carried a snapshot of him sitting on a dead tiger, but the camera must have slipped because he looked as if he had no teeth and an enormous nose with a little extra one beside it. We never asked her about that because Nan and I got some funny pictures sometimes with our Brownie, too. One puzzled us for a long time, it was all wavy hills and white dots with Nan's foot down in one corner.

The week before Christmas was so exciting that every morning when I woke up I lay quite still for a minute, trying to guess what was going to happen that day.

A very special occasion was when Cook invited me to go down to the kitchen after breakfast. I'd had a bilious attack when everyone else stirred the enormous bowl of Christmas pudding mixture, making a wish for each month in the year, so she thought the next best thing would be for me to look at the twenty-four finished puddings in their white basins. I had no idea what a kitchen would be like, and when I got as far as the green-baize door I was shivering. Then Charlesworth came along smiling and pushed the door open so that we went together down the steep, dark stairs to the basement.

It was difficult to see much at first, it was so far down below the pavement, and there were thick net curtains over the window as well as black bars to keep out burglars. But there was a cheerful fire roaring away in the middle of a long black stove, and shining copper pans all down one wall. Cook was sitting in a wicker armchair drinking a cup of tea, and on her lap she held a black cat who was fast asleep. My shivers and shyness vanished: I'd been praying for a kitten every evening for weeks and all the time there was one right here, in our very own house! I knelt on the floor beside Cook and stroked him, hardly able to wait to carry him up to the Nursery to show Nan. But:

'No, no, Miss Diana.' Cook's voice always sounded as if she'd just eaten pots and pots of jam. 'He lives down here. You see, he has to catch mice as reg'lar as you has to go to school.'

After that it wasn't easy to be interested in twenty-four white pudding basins with linen caps on, but I so much wanted to be invited down to the kitchen again that I said they were beautiful. Then Charlesworth said she was going to ask Grannie if I could have a taste of pudding this year instead of jelly; and if so she'd make sure I got a piece with a sixpence in it.

Nan and I never went to the Park during that week at all, we were too busy going by bus to some of the big London shops to buy Grannie's Christmas presents for her. We never had Christmas decorations at home because Grandpapa said they might catch fire, but the shops made up for it. There were life-size pictures of Father Christmas and his reindeer, tinsel, fairy-lights, coloured paper bells as big as our Nursery table, and even the boxes of hand-kerchiefs we bought for Cook and Charlesworth had little gold wreaths and imitation holly stuck on the lids.

This treat came our way because Aunt Clare had her eye on someone again; before, she'd always bought Grannie's Christmas presents. He was a young painter with greasy black hair that came down over his collar; he had no money so he was staying with cousins who lived two houses away from us, and he spent all day in the Square Garden painting dull things like the iron seats and the rusty lawnroller. Aunt Clare stopped washing her hair every week, wore strings of wooden beads and went out quite early every morning with a Thermos and sandwiches to sit beside him all day. Nan and I hoped it was going to go well for her at last, and we thought it might because even her voice had changed this time, getting boomy and soft. Whenever she saw us going by, she used to call through the railings: 'Hello, Scrap,' or 'Have a nice walk, Nan dear,' which made us jump until we got used to it.

But three days before Christmas, when Great-Uncle Patrick and his wife Great-Aunt Madge were coming to lunch, Charlesworth found a note in the letterbox addressed to Aunt Clare. It was from the Painter and said not to bother to bring out any sandwiches for him today because he'd left for Paris where he was going to live in a garret and Starve for his Art. Folded inside was a signed sketch of the Square Garden toolshed.

Aunt Clare went straight to bed with a bad headache and Grannie was in a great fuss. She felt she ought to be dabbing Aunt Clare's forehead with eau-de-Cologne and making helpful suggestions for the future, but at the same time she hadn't seen Great-Uncle Patrick for five years. In the end Great-Uncle Patrick won and Nan offered to sit with Aunt Clare during lunch if I could have mine in the dining-room.

Great-Uncle Patrick was a disappointment. Probably after the magic birds on our nursery screen, the ebony legs and all the brass gongs he'd sent, I expected him to be *different*. He wasn't. Very tall and thin, he had a sad, yellowy-white moustache and little pale eyes that looked as if they'd been crying.

But Great-Aunt Madge more than made up for him. She was small and fat and wore a bright orange wig that wasn't on quite straight, so that wispy bits of her own grey hair stuck out at one side and round the back. She had a huge collar of silver coins round the neck of her rather dusty black jersey, and more coins dangled from her ears. Her little podgy hands were grubby, but as she had at least three beautiful rings on every finger she obviously couldn't be bothered to keep taking them off just to wash. Every time she moved, which was often, weird creaking noises came from her middle (Nan said afterwards that it must have been 'her stays, poor thing'), and she never stopped talking. Grannie and Great-Uncle Patrick sat together on the sofa holding hands, looking like two shy children who've come to the wrong party.

I'm not sure exactly when I was certain that Grannie didn't like Great-Aunt Madge, but it was before we went down to lunch. Anyway, I simply loved her. She even made being seasick on the voyage home sound funny as she waved her hands and creaked away, while her wig wobbled so much I thought it would fall off if she laughed any more.

She went on talking all through lunch so that Grannie forgot and gave me a big helping of duck and roast potatoes. I was going to remind her when Charlesworth, behind Great-Uncle Patrick's chair, winked and put a finger to her lips. Next time she passed the sideboard she whisked my hot-plate of fish away, and so I ate the most wonderful meal I'd ever tasted. The only trouble was, I'd have liked to be absolutely quiet so that I could taste the duck – and, at the same time, not have to chew at all while I was laughing at Great-Aunt Madge's jokes. But you can't have everything.

After lunch Great-Uncle Patrick gave me a ten-shilling note and Great-Aunt Madge, after thinking she'd lost it in her big embroidered handbag, found a coral necklace she had brought for me.

I forgot all about the Painter in my anxiety to find Nan and tell her everything, so I burst into Aunt Clare's bedroom holding out my splendid presents and shouting: 'Look! Oh, Nan, look what they gave me!'

Nan's warning 'Ssh' came too late from the corner where she was sitting in the darkened room.

'How can you be so selfish, Diana. I was almost asleep.'

Aunt Clare's voice had lost its boominess and gone flat and cross again. 'Did her wig fall off?' she added unexpectedly.

'Not quite.' I began to giggle. 'Perhaps it will on Christmas Day, though.' But I'd gone too far. That was the trouble with Aunt Clare. One minute she was so friendly, and the next so snappy that it was really safer just to answer Yes or No.

'Cheeky little brat! For God's sake take her out of my room, Nan,' she said. 'Although I can't imagine what Mother is thinking of, letting That Woman come into this house, that's no excuse for you to be rude, Diana!'

Safely up in the Nursery, Nan helped me to put on my corals and then we sat down to make a list. I usually made all my Christmas presents, a felt penwiper for Grandpapa, a pincushion for Grannie and a bookmarker for Aunt Clare. Grannie always bought expensive presents for me to send to Mother and Daddy and something extra-special for me to give Nan. But with ten whole shillings to spend I wanted to buy all the presents this year. We'd get our coats and go straight along to Woolworth's, Nan promised; the money would stretch nicely over my whole list there.

'Why shouldn't Grannie let Great-Aunt Madge come to the house?' I asked suddenly. The list had put it out of my mind for a few minutes.

'Oh, I don't know, darling,' Nan answered, getting down our outdoor things. 'I expect people do funny things in those hot climates sometimes . . . but your Great-Uncle Patrick is a proper gentleman.' With which completely baffling answer I had to be content.

I couldn't get to sleep for hours on Christmas Eve. We always put a Thermos of cocoa and two digestive biscuits on our best pink saucer in the fender for Father Christmas. And this year, being so rich, I'd bought him a hanky with an Irish shamrock in the corner, as well. I noticed Nan using a hanky just like it a few days later and she said: Wasn't it funny how great minds always think alike?

Because Nanny Warriss had given her one exactly the same for Christmas!

I must have fallen asleep eventually, though, because suddenly it was time to wake up. It was still dark but I knew it must be morning because, when I crept out to look, the biscuits and hanky had gone and the Thermos was empty. Above all, hanging on the brass knob of my bed was the bulgy, shadowy shape of Grandpapa's long fishing-stocking simply full of presents from Father Christmas. He'd even put a golliwog looking out of the top, like the one I'd admired so much in Woolworth's the other day – and this was really clever of him, because it wasn't on the list I'd sent up the chimney two weeks ago.

Nan let me put the light on but said she simply couldn't wake up herself as it was only half past five, so she turned over and pulled the bedclothes over her head. I didn't mind. There was a queer excitement about opening surprises all alone while everyone else was asleep. I played for about an hour, then, after arranging everything for Nan to see, I went back to bed with my new golliwog.

All the big, family presents were exchanged much later in the day, but Nan and I had Nursery breakfast and gave each other our private ones then. She had knitted me a lovely pair of bright red gloves with flowers embroidered on the backs, and we were both so excited about the surprise I'd bought for her when she wasn't looking that we couldn't think of anything to say – we just stared at it. It was an evening comb in a pink case for parties. The case had bright, glinty diamonds all round the edge and there were tiny ones stuck all the way up the back of the comb, too. Nan said it was the most beautiful thing she'd ever seen. Then, at last, she put it carefully away in her handbag.

I was so longing to see Great-Aunt Felicity again that I fidgeted all through the last hymn in church and Grandpapa had to lean behind Grannie to tap me gently on the shoulder with his spectacle-case several times. But I didn't mind because his eyes were twinkling as if he understood.

And when we got back from church Charlesworth opened the front door immediately, looking quite flustered and pleased, to tell us that Miss Felicity and Mister Bart were here already, waiting in the drawing-room.

I flew upstairs ahead of everybody else and flung myself at Great-Aunt Felicity, hugging and kissing her and making her promise to have tea with us in the Nursery. Then I remembered Great-Uncle Bart.

He was standing behind us, grinning down at me. He was ugly, much worse than he'd looked in the snapshot, with no teeth as far as I could see; and he *had* got a second nose – only the second one was really a bump with three long, black hairs growing out of it.

By the time the gong sounded for lunch, the drawing-room was so full of relations, all talking and laughing and drinking cherry brandy out of crystal glasses, that I felt giddy and sat down on the low, blue velvet praying-chair by the fire.

'Don't burn your legs, child,' Great-Aunt Gussie roared at me, fixing her monocle in to peer at my mottled bare knees. 'Gives you scorch marks. Hideous. Not that they'll make much difference to you.' She dropped her monocle and turned back to Great-Uncle Patrick.

'A little of what you fancy does a *lot* of good at Christmas,' carolled Great-Aunt Madge as she made for the door, bracelets and necklaces a-jingle and her wig at a most precarious angle. Great-Uncle Joe's eye twitched away merrily and, to my enthralled horror, he turned and caught Great-Aunt Fidge by her arm before he remembered! She shrank back against the wall, her bright, witchy eyes tight shut behind the layers of veiling, and when we all got down to the dining-room she asked to have a place laid for her separately, on a small card table by the window, in case anyone touched her again.

Sitting on an upright wooden chair from the spare room, wedged between Grannie and Great-Aunt Felicity, I felt I could burst with happiness. But Great-Aunt Gussie stared across at me just then and I thought bursting might be even more nuisance than being sick, so I squeezed Great-Aunt Felicity's hand hard under the tablecloth.

By the time Grandpapa had carved the big turkey and doled out the little brown sausages and bacon rolls, Charlesworth had been round the table several times, filling up glasses. Great-Aunt Madge and Great-Uncle Bart were having such a lovely time, laughing and nudging each other, that watching them made me laugh, too.

'Don't laugh, Diana, it's horrible,' Great-Aunt Felicity whispered. Her pretty face was white and her eyes full of tears. I'd never seen a grown-up crying before and now, for Nan's and my dearest friend to be upset on this special day was more than I could bear. Throwing my arms round her waist, I caught the edge of my plate with my elbow and tipped gravy and bits of turkey all over the cloth.

'Dear, *dear* Great-Aunt Felicity, don't cry,' I begged, kissing her neck which was as high as I could reach. 'They're going to pull crackers in the kitchen and Nan's promised to save the paper hats – you shall have them *all*, I promise, and – '

Grannie was gently pulling me back on to my chair while Charlesworth put a clean napkin under my plate to hide the worst of the mess. Everybody had stopped talking. Great-Uncle Bart suddenly leant over the table and said :

'You – little girl – what'sh yer name ?'

'Diana,' giggled Great-Aunt Madge.

'Diana, then. Don't let Felishity depress you. She de-preshes me, even at Chr-Chrishtmas !'

Grannie's hand was pressing my arm, telling me not to answer, and across my head I heard her whisper to her sister : 'Don't worry, darling, Matthew will look after him later.'

'He'll be deathly ill before lunch is over, Elizabeth. I know he will.'

Matthew was Grandpapa's name and, as everyone started talking at once, I wondered what was going to happen. Great-Uncle Bart looked quite well even though the hairy bump by his nose had gone bright red, and all he did was keep on laughing more than ever with Great-Aunt Madge.

Was it *possible* that laughing too much could make you die? The idea was so frightening I began to shiver. Nan and I laughed a lot every week when we read *Tiger Tim* and *Puck*, but we mustn't even look at them again, and I had to find Nan, quickly, and warn her. Even the promise of a taste of plum pudding with a sixpence in it didn't matter any more.

They weren't going to have their Christmas dinner in the kitchen until we'd finished in the dining-room, so at this very minute Nan might be looking at *Tiger Tim* while she waited, and laughing herself to death all alone upstairs.

Grannie was talking to Great-Uncle Joe and I could hardly see Grandpapa at the other end of the table, there were so many silver dishes, glasses and bowls of holly between us. But I *had* to get permission to get down and run and find Nan. I'd forgotten Great-Aunt Fidge behind us until she said:

'The child is going to be sick again, Elizabeth!'

'Oh, Lord!' Aunt Clare rushed round the table and jerked my chair back so quickly we both bumped into Great-Aunt Fidge's card table; she made a funny mewing noise and pulled one of the heavy red plush curtains right round her.

'Children ought never to be let out of the Nursery,' boomed Great-Aunt Gussie.

I didn't care. While Aunt Clare put things straight on the card table I seized my chance and ran out of the room. Charlesworth was outside, waiting to hand round second helpings.

'Lor', Miss Diana. Not having one of your bad turns, are you? Christmas Day and all?'

'No, but I *must* see Nan, it's dreadfully important.'

'Well, maybe you're best out of the dining-room before Miss Felicity's husband gets any worse,' she said. 'Lifting his elbow like that, and in your grandparents' house, too!'

'It isn't his elbow, it's laughing that's going to kill him, Great-Aunt Felicity said so. That's why I must find Nan. Where is she?'

'You shouldn't go in, not really, not till they're ready.

Still, I daresay no one will be any the wiser. She's in the drawing-room, setting out the presents.'

I flew up the stairs. If Nan was busy she wouldn't have looked at *Tiger Tim* again, but she might have it with her.

The family always opened their Christmas presents after lunch, but as I'd never been allowed to have it in the dining-room before, all the exciting parcels were usually arranged round the big sofa by the time Nan brought me down to open mine. Now half of them were still on the floor and Nan was trying to balance a great big one on the back of the sofa. She wasn't laughing.

'Diana! You mustn't look!'

I hugged her very tight and told her we must never, never laugh very much again, and it might be safer if we didn't buy *Tiger Tim* or *Puck* any more. It was lovely sitting there, close together, with the Christmas presents all round us while I told her everything that had happened in the dining-room. Nan still hadn't seen Great-Uncle Bart but she said she knew laughing never hurt anybody so it couldn't be that. We were still wondering what it *could* be that was going to make him so ill when I remembered what Charles-worth had said about lifting his elbow.

'Perhaps we'd better not do that,' I suggested when I'd repeated it to Nan. 'Though it'll make brushing our hair and all that awfully difficult.'

A minute later Charlesworth came in with a little tray. She was hobbling badly and all the lines on her face were turned down, but I knew she was trying to smile.

'A promise is a promise, Miss. And it's got a sixpence in it!'

The little wedge of Christmas pudding was on one of Grannie's special, gold-edged plates and there was a crested spoon beside it. It was much too beautiful to eat.

'You have it, darling,' urged Nan. 'We shan't get our tea much before bed-time today.' She and Charlesworth went just outside the door for a quick chat, but I couldn't eat the pudding. Only I didn't want to hurt Charlesworth so I got my clean hanky out of the leg of my knickers and wrapped the pudding up carefully. Nan and I would find the sixpence in it later on in the Nursery, and then we should be able to visit Woolworth's again.

When Nan came back she was too flustered to notice how clean my plate was. If we didn't hurry up the parcels wouldn't be arranged before everyone came upstairs. So I handed her the presents while she put them round the sofa.

'That's my brooch from Mother and Daddy,' I said, passing her a small registered envelope addressed to me. I got one every year and this would be the fifth one to keep in our washstand drawer. They were always long, thin gold bars with either the letter 'D' at one end or a little bird or butterfly. However hard we tried to pin them on to my white blouses, they looked lop-sided and the important bit got hidden under the collar.

'Never mind,' said Nan. 'There are some lovely fat parcels with your name on as well.'

We'd nearly finished when I picked up a funny one wrapped in red, creased paper that must have been used before. It had my name scrawled across it and I felt it cautiously.

'Oh, Nan! It's a doll!' We stared at each other, horrified.

'And it's from your Great-Aunt Madge,' Nan said. 'Diana, don't get upset. Leave it till last and bring it straight upstairs. She means well.'

The drawing-room was full of people. Only Great-Uncle Bart wasn't there, and Great-Aunt Felicity's eyes were very red and she stayed close to Grannie.

Paper crackled about all over the room as everyone opened their parcels. I had two fluffy dogs, a pink Teddy-bear, a set of battledore and shuttlecock (which Nan and I had been wishing for for ages) and, of course, the brooch from Mother and Daddy. But best of all was a miniature Chinese gong from Great-Uncle Patrick with a little hammer covered in soft leather. It made a tiny, muffled sound, high up, and I couldn't stop trying it; I was putting off opening Great-Aunt Madge's doll. Then, swooping down on me, her

wig over one ear, she said:

'Open mine, Diana. She's not much, but at least she's come all the way from Hong-Kong.'

I shut my eyes as I tore off the creased, red wrapping. If it was a horrid, dead lady with black hair like the one Daddy brought, not even Jesus Tender Shepherd Hear Me would be able to prevent me screaming. All the others had finished looking at their things and were watching me.

As the paper came off, I smelt her. Better than my old panama hat, better than any smell in the whole world. Betsy Caroline was made of cork with a round, flat face, fawn darning-wool stitched in to make her hair and black for her eyes; her mouth was painted on to match the red-and-white checked calico dress she wore, and her legs and arms stretched straight out without hands or feet. I loved her so much I didn't know what to do – but I was sure I'd guessed her name right and that she was pleased.

'You can take her into your bath, if you still play with bath toys.' Great-Aunt Madge sounded as if she was apologizing for her present, somehow. 'I didn't realize you were nearly six now.'

'It'll need a good wash if you bought it in Hong-Kong,' snorted Great-Aunt Gussie. 'Bound to be full of germs!'

I left the fluffy dogs – even the battledore and shuttle-cock – and ran out of the room, clutching Betsy Caroline against my chest as if someone was going to part us. Nan hadn't come up to the Nursery yet after her own Christmas dinner, but for the first time it didn't feel so lonely there without her. Nowhere was ever going to feel really lonely any more.

But I felt dreadful next morning when Grannie, pale and tired after the family Christmas, said: 'You never thanked Great-Aunt Madge, Diana. I think she was very hurt. You see, coming from abroad, she couldn't be expected to remember that you're getting quite a big girl now.'

'Oh, Grannie! *Surely* she understood that I loved Betsy Caroline far more than all my other things? I hadn't time to hug her or say thank you in case Great-Aunt Gussie went on about germs and tried to take Betsy Caroline away before we could be safe in the Nursery!'

'Safe in the Nursery,' Grannie repeated sadly. Then she put her arms round me, forgetting about Great-Aunt Madge. 'This must seem a very big, frightening house for a child.'

I clung to her, terrified. If she really thought that, she might send me away.

'Grannie, promise – promise, *promise* you won't send Nan and me away? This is a lovely house, even Grandpapa's study, and – and – the linen cupboard as long as the light's on. Nan and I wouldn't be happy without our special things . . . our flying-bird screen and – and – the beautiful table mat her sister crocheted us for Christmas. Please, *please* promise . . .'

She hugged me very tightly. 'Of course I'm not going to send you away, darling.'

It was comforting. Because Grannie kept her promises and Nan and I would be safe. The one thing I never even dreamed of was that I might ever have to be without Nan.

PART THREE

Far from being sent away, Nan and I hardly left the Nursery at all during the next three months. In January I caught measles at school. It began like an ordinary headache, only soon there was a sore throat as well and queer hot-and-cold shivers, even in bed. Then the dreams started and although I screamed and screamed, I couldn't wake up or make Nan hear: there was sand everywhere, thick, bright sand that hurt my eyes terribly though I knew they were really shut. And soldiers. They were in scarlet with black fluffy hats like the ones outside Buckingham Palace, but they were all so tall I couldn't see their faces properly and their marching was horrible. They began at the top of my left eye and went down to the corner of my right, and every time they stamped their feet green sparks flew out of the sand and I could feel their boots thumping inside my head.

Suddenly they all tumbled down on top of one another and began rolling very slowly over and over until they fell out of my right eye and the sand grew darker.

'It looks as if our Sleeping Beauty's going to wake.' It was Dr McLain's voice, miles and miles away.

'Oh, I do hope so, Doctor. Three days and nights now she's been in delirium.'

Nan! She was there at last and I tried to call out, to explain that I was in a desert and not in Delirium at all, otherwise she'd go looking for me in the wrong place.

No words would come because my mouth was full of sand, but I just managed to open my eyes, though they felt gritty and sore too. It was dark and shadowy and the Nursery door had disappeared. Instead a thick blanket was hanging where it ought to have been.

Dr McLain bent down and listened to my chest, and at last I saw Nan standing behind him. It was funny that she'd come to find me in her blue flannel dressing-gown with her hair down in plaits, but I had to warn her about the soldiers – they were probably hiding behind that blanket. Then Dr McLain stood up, holding my wrist, and I forgot the soldiers because, with his head out of the way, I saw Grannie sitting in the rocking-chair by the fire. *Grannie in the Nursery!* It had never happened before so I knew I was still dreaming. Besides, somebody seemed to have washed my hair and bathed me in my nightie while I was asleep, only they hadn't dried me – everything was sopping.

'You'll do now, young lady,' Dr McLain was saying. 'Have a good snooze and feel quite perky by morning. And you get some rest yourself, Nan.' He turned away from the bed and Grannie stood up.

'I will, Doctor. Once I've changed her bed and dried her hair a bit.' Poor Nan, she must be feeling awful at putting me to bed all wet. Perhaps the linen cupboard bulb had broken and she couldn't find a towel in the dark. I longed to hug and comfort her . . . but she was going further and further away . . .

Although measles itself only lasted about a week, Nan and I had to stay in quarantine for two more, with the blanket over our door. Nan wasn't even allowed to go down and have her supper in the kitchen because although she'd had measles, Maisie hadn't, and Dr McLain said Nan might Carry Germs.

We wondered a lot about germs and how you could carry something you couldn't see. At first we thought they might be tiny black caterpillars that hid in your clothes and jumped out on to people when they weren't looking. But in the end we decided they must be bad fairies, covered with spots, who became invisible the minute they'd covered you with spots too. It made sense but it was worrying. Suppose they flew round the blanket when Nan had to open the door to go down and boil a kettle in the bathroom? Then they would hide on the stairs until Maisie went up to bed, and catch her that way.

We didn't worry very often, though, because we were so busy. Nan taught me to knit, and from scraps of coloured wool in her knitting-bag I made Betsy Caroline three new dresses. The first one was dark green, left over from Grannie's new hot-water bottle cover, and the holes where stitches got dropped looked just like flowers if you half shut your eyes. The next had to be navy because Nan was un-picking an old jersey that was too small, but the third was simply beautiful. It was scarlet, with yellow stripes from the wool Nan had used for my Christmas gloves. Luckily the five stitches I dropped in that one were all in the same place, so we decided to put the dress on back-to-front and then Betsy Caroline wouldn't notice.

More exciting still, I now got little packets by post which Charlesworth hid in her apron pocket until she brought up our breakfast tray. Newspapers had always been forbidden in the Nursery, because Grandpapa believed they were bad for children. But with poor Nan a prisoner because of Maisie not getting germs, he decided that she should be allowed the *Daily Mail*. And so free samples came into our lives.

On nearly every page there were advertisements with coupons in the corner. Nan lent me her pen with the view of St Paul's Cathedral on the handle, and a bottle of ink, and I filled in my name and address very neatly and addressed the envelopes carefully so they shouldn't get lost in the post. Through being ill I'd saved up my pocket-money, so when Nan went out for her hour's walk every afternoon, she bought the stamps and popped the letters in the pillar box.

Nan let Charlesworth in on our secret because – although there was nothing wrong in it – Grandpapa mightn't like finding little boxes of face-powder and catalogues for corsets among his important letters every morning.

The face-powder was the best of all. There were three colours – Natural, Pink and a yellowy one called Rachelle –

so I sent for them in turn and they arrived in dear little mauve boxes the size of a shilling. Nan made miniature powder puffs out of cottonwool and we spent hours trying to decide which colour suited us best. There were baby packets of seeds, too, so we grew mustard and cress on saucers, and one week I got a sample bunion pad for Charlesworth and she said it eased her a lot.

The corset catalogue came later, after we were out of quarantine. It was lucky I hadn't sent for it sooner because, on the last day of quarantine, Dr McLain came and told Nan that any papers or magazines I'd touched ought to be burnt and all my toys must be baked in Cook's oven for three hours. After that, he said, we should have to order the Man with the Bermolene Candle.

Cook got very cross about the toys. It was her Baking Day, when she made her special muffins and sponge cakes, and so now what was she expected to do? Send up a load of old, hot toys to the drawing-room at tea-time instead? Besides, they were going to make her kitchen smell something shocking. But Nan promised to take them down very first thing in the morning while Maisie was safely upstairs making beds, then they'd all be done before it was time for elevenses.

I could hardly wait for the Man with the Bermolene Candle. It was such a magic-sounding name I wasn't sure whether to expect him on a flying carpet, dressed like Aladdin and carrying a beautiful rainbow candle, or riding a camel wearing long white robes like a picture in the Beginner's Geography Book.

'What's a Bermolene Candle for?' I asked Nan.

'To disinfect everything, darling – our beds and pillows, in fact everything that's been in the Nursery while you were ill. I'm afraid it smells very nasty and makes your eyes water, but as soon as he's finished I'll open the window wide before we go to bed.'

After that I knew he wouldn't be coming in a magic way, just with a horse and cart like everyone else. But there wasn't time to be disappointed because we were in what Nan called 'one of our flusters' that morning. To be dressed, and have the room tidy for the Bermolene Candle Man, as well as getting my toys down to Cook before Grandpapa read prayers, we had to get up a whole hour early. Nan always dressed underneath her long winceyette nightie, using it like a tent until her petticoat was on properly. Only that morning she was in such a hurry that everything seemed to get stuck or twisted, so I shut my eyes tight in case the nightie slipped. It didn't, but she kept saying:

'We'll be at sixes and sevens all day long, I know we shall.'

We weren't, though it felt funny having our breakfast on a card table in the linen room. Then the Speaking Tube whistled and it was Charlesworth to say the Man was on his way up. When he got as far as our stairs I ran out on to the landing to look because he was making such a funny noise – like hopping. There was a 'clomp', then nothing, and another 'clomp'. I forgot that it's rude to stare because, while one leg had an ordinary foot and everything, the other was straight and stuck out of his trouser leg just like Betsy Caroline's! I'd always *known* she was real and now, perhaps if I prayed very hard, she might grow feet like me – or my legs might turn into cork like hers. Either way, at least we'd be the same.

'*Is* it cork?' I asked the Man eagerly. This was far more important than saying good morning.

'Matter of fact, Miss, it is.' He'd got to the top by then and he had the bluest eyes and the saddest moustache I'd ever seen: the browny-yellow part came right down over his mouth while the long grey ends straggled on to his collar.

'Diana, that's very rude.' Nan was just behind me. 'You know you must never make personal remarks.'

I held her hand so that she would share the excitement. 'It wasn't a personal remark, Nan. It's the most important thing in the world. Look, he's got a cork leg like Betsy Caroline, which means I could have two if we pray a lot.'

'Oh, Diana, you and your imagination!' she said, but she wasn't cross any more. 'This is the room for the Candle,' she told the Man, and I noticed a small green baize bag in his hand.

'It must be a very small Candle to fit in there.'

'Small but thorough, Miss. Watch me set it up if you like.' The yellowy bit of his moustache whooshed in and out as he breathed and I wondered how he ever managed to eat anything. If he had to hold the moustache up all the time, then he wouldn't have a spare hand to hold a knife *and* fork . . . I wished I'd sent for a free sample of something called 'Saverol – a good, nourishing meal, just add boiling water and drink whenever you feel low.' As Nan and I had Horlicks every night I hadn't bothered, but it might have helped the Candle Man. Except if it was sticky his moustache would get in an awful mess, so perhaps he was better holding it up after all.

The Candle was very dull, more like a night-light, and he stood it in the middle of the floor in a dark-green enamel holder.

'There,' he said as he lit it. 'Burn for eight hours and you'll not have a germ in the place. I'll come for the holder four-thirty sharp.'

He clomp-hop-clomped his way downstairs on his splendid cork leg but already a horrible smell was seeping out under the Nursery door.

'It's a beautiful day,' Nan said. 'I'll pop down and ask Grannie if we can go for a short walk and then have lunch in the Study afterwards.'

'But our hats and coats are in there!'

It looked as if the sixes and sevens were catching up with us after all. We had to spend all day down in Grandpapa's study to get away from the smell, but at least we were able to play Snap because there were some playing cards in the drawer of the drawing-room table which Grannie said we could use. The parrot never woke up at all.

Great-Aunt Gussie arrived to visit Grannie and saw us while we were waiting in the hall for my toys to be brought up from the kitchen.

'Diana?' She screwed in her monocle and looked me over. 'Good heavens, child, you're Skinny Lizzie from Bone Yard. Need to put on a bit of flesh, eh?'

68

Secretly I'd been thinking the same thing myself. Grannie and Aunt Clare – even Nan – had nice, soft bulgy bits on their chests which I envied. My own chest was so flat I could see the ribs sticking out and, after Great-Aunt Gussie's remark, I suddenly realized that they all had something else I hadn't got either – corsets. If I sent off for the free catalogue about corsets then surely I'd find the answer.

Unfortunately the Bermolene Candle smell was so strong that Nan and I slept with the Nursery window wide open, top and bottom, for three nights. We couldn't have stayed in there otherwise, it was such a sickly-sweet smell that shut the back of your nose and made your eyes smart. And on the fourth morning I felt hot and had a sore throat. Dr McLain came upstairs and said :

'Ha! Opened the window and In Flew Enza, I see.'

So, once more, Nan and I were shut up in the Nursery, though we didn't have to have a blanket over the door. But she was allowed to have the *Daily Mail* again so I filled in the coupon for the corset catalogue. Nan was surprised when I gave her the envelope and the penny out of my moneybox for a stamp.

'Diana, you don't need corsets, darling. You've got your Liberty Bodices, so don't waste your money.'

'I want it,' I said stubbornly, hugging Betsy Caroline who had gone toast-colour after being baked. Her checked calico dress was a bit scorched round the edge, too, but she smelt lovely.

'Well, I suppose a catalogue can't do any harm.' Nan sounded doubtful and looked as if she hoped I'd explain. Only, for the first time I couldn't tell her what was worrying me. Because no one ever talked about them, the bulges I longed for instinctively seemed private – as private as going alone to look for a baby or dressing decently under a nightie.

When it arrived at last, the catalogue was wonderful; pages and pages of shiny paper full of pictures of ladies laced up like bolsters. They all appeared to be wearing corsets over pretty, flimsy party dresses but I hadn't time to think about that – I was only interested in their chests. Then

I found what I was looking for; underneath a lady with two egg cups sticking out in front it said : 'Padded brassière to give size and uplift.'

Cottonwool! *That's* what they all wore inside their clothes!

That evening, after Nan had gone down for her supper, I crept out of bed and opened our washstand drawer. There was a spare tube of toothpaste, grey powders and one teeny piece of cottonwool that wouldn't do to make a bulge at all.

I knew that cottonwool wasn't very expensive although Mr Maloney tied it up just as carefully as he did Grannie's medicine. But what excuse could I give for wanting to buy a whole roll myself? I was bothering God on and off all day about my cork legs, but I didn't think He'd forget them if I slipped in a quick word about the cottonwool. He was my only hope, really.

I quite understood that cork legs might take some time – He probably had to send away for them or even have them specially made. But He obviously knew all about Mr Maloney's shop, and how easy it would be, because He answered the cottonwool prayer so quickly I had to pay a special visit to the lavatory to thank Him. I couldn't very well kneel down in the Nursery without telling Nan why; and once Aunt Clare had caught me having a quick pray for the cork legs on the bathroom stairs and said in a sneery voice : 'Good God – first twitches, now religious mania, what on earth will you get next?' So the lavatory was the only private place in an emergency.

It all happened because Nan had met Nanny Warriss on her walk the very day after my prayer and Nanny Warriss had said : 'It's a shame Diana's had to miss so much school. Miss Dolly, the Head, was saying what a lovely old Toy-maker she'd have made in the little play they're doing at the end of term. Deborah's to be a Fairy doll.'

As soon as she'd told me this Nan gave her special smile for surprises and brought a beautiful parcel out of her big handbag, done up with Mr Maloney's pale blue string and sealing-wax.

'So I began thinking,' she said as I tore open the paper

to make quite sure what was inside. 'You're much, much better now and, if it's fine tomorrow, I don't see why you shouldn't go out for a little and go back to school next Monday. Then you'll be in good time for the play! And I expect the Toymaker is supposed to be a very old man, so I bought some cottonwool so's we can make a big, fluffy beard!'

'Oh, Nan,' I hugged her very tight. 'I'll draw lots and lots of beards to see which looks best – then we can make it tomorrow!'

After I'd thanked God for His prompt reply I added a promise; I didn't need very large bulges or my shirt blouses wouldn't do up and they were new, so I would faithfully keep enough cottonwool for the beard even if it had to be rather a wispy one.

I studied the corset catalogue very carefully during my afternoon rest and planned exactly how it must be done. I could hardly wait for Nan's supper-time. She'd be so proud of me for finding out this grown-up thing all by myself!

The moment she left the Nursery, I began. First, I stuffed two of Betsy Caroline's knitted dresses with the cotton-wool, tying them round at each end with darning wool so it couldn't fall out. Then, with more wool, I joined them to-gether quite loosely – they really looked just like the egg cups in the catalogue, and nobody would ever see that one was green and the other navy. But after that it got harder. I'd kept Mr Maloney's pale blue string, cut it in half, and now I tied one piece to each of the bulges and struggled and struggled to tie the ends together behind my back. The bulges kept slipping down round my tummy and the bits of string *wouldn't* tie properly. My throat began to hurt again and I suddenly remembered about not lifting my elbow like Uncle Bart right in the middle, which made things much more difficult.

Only just in time I managed a sort of granny-knot, pulled my nightie on again and, by keeping my arms tightly against the string at each side, stood ready as Nan came through the door.

'Diana! What *are* you doing out of bed?' she said. 'And

standing there bang in a draught after all the trouble we've had!'

I turned a little more sideways so she *must* see the bulges.

'Oh, dear. I know you've been up to something. What on earth have you got under your nightie?'

'A proper chest – like yours, and Aunt Clare's and everybody.'

Dear, dear Nan. I wasn't sure whether she was laughing or crying, but she said: 'Come on, hop into bed and cuddle down warm, then you can tell me all about it,' and she tucked me in and sat beside me. The woolly dresses were scratchy against my skin and the clumsy knot in the string was rubbing my back. I started to cry as I told her everything.

Very gently Nan pulled back the bedclothes, rolled me over and untied my creation. 'They're lovely, Diana,' she said as she made me cosy again. 'But, you know, you mustn't hurry to grow up before you have to. In a few years' time your own chest will begin to grow little bulges by itself, just the way we grew the mustard and cress. It'll grow so slowly it won't scratch or tickle at all, in fact it won't hurt a bit. Just you wait and see. Now I think we could both do with a nice, hot drink.'

Next morning I was covered with little blisters. Not from the string. I had chicken-pox.

Spending another three weeks in the Nursery gave me lots of time to go on praying for cork legs. I particularly wanted them before the summer holidays. Then, if we went to the sea as Nan thought we might, I'd be able to float about with Betsy Caroline even though I couldn't swim.

But when I was better and we were expecting the Bermolene Candle Man again, a dreadful thing happened. On her way up to bed with the tea-set in a baize bag under one arm and Petty under the other, Charlesworth stopped to rest her feet on our landing and Nan went out for a goodnight chat. She didn't quite shut our door and I heard Charlesworth saying:

'Must count our blessings, mustn't we?' She had a good wheeze and a cough. 'Leastways with me it's only bunions. But that poor man coming tomorrow, now. Says his cork leg plays him up something terrible in wet weather – and to think the Germans shot off his own. Great one for playing football, he was. Before the Germans got him.'

I saw it all so vividly I dived down and pulled the bed-clothes right over my head to stop hearing any more. God had sent the cottonwool so quick – suppose my cork legs were waiting and He sent the Germans to shoot off my own so as to be ready for them? The only thing I knew about Germans was that they had killed Aunt Clare and Mother's only brother before I was born, and Nan once told me never to ask Grannie or Grandpapa about Germans as they got upset.

Now they'd be coming right into our home and it was all my fault. I was too frightened to pray, too frightened to do anything except hug Betsy Caroline so tight that a little piece of cork came off the side of her face.

When Nan came back I pretended to be asleep. When the Germans came looking for me, they mightn't hurt her if she didn't know anything about it.

Next morning I had a high temperature and Nan carried me down to the horrid spare room while the Bermolene Candle Man did his disinfecting.

'H'm,' said Dr McLain. 'Influenza *again*, Diana? Giving

73

everyone a lot of trouble, aren't you?' But his voice was kind and he and Nan went into the corner and had a long talk about Aspirins and Grey Powders. I wanted to tell them I was only ill because of waiting for the Germans, but Nan would have had to tell Grannie and it would make her cry I was getting hotter and hotter when I suddenly thought of Jennie and Mr Anstruther in the factory. Jenny was never afraid of anything, even before she knew that Mr Anstruther would fling open the factory door and start the lovely happy ending for her. I shut my eyes so as to see them both better, and began to plan the sort of palace they would live in . . .

Nan and I spent a week in the spare room until all the Bermolene Candle fumes had blown out of the Nursery. I hated the huge double bed where I kept losing Betsy Caroline, who had gone the colour of Nan's brown outdoor shoes after being baked again in the oven. And poor Nan had to sleep on a long, curly-topped sofa. I begged her to come into the big bed but she always said she was quite comfortable.

By about the fifth day the Germans got a bit hazy – I'd no idea what they looked like, anyway, and they didn't seem to be coming. Dr McLain said:

'Mending nicely now, eh? What you and Nan need is a good breath of sea air.'

We never got it.

At the end of the week I woke up very early feeling so well I jumped out of bed to wake Nan so we could make our early tea. I kissed her, pulled down the blankets, but she didn't open her eyes. She was white and her face was wet. I ran next door into Grannie and Grandpapa's bedroom without even knocking.

'Nan's dead!' I screamed. 'Oh, *do* something – come quickly . . .'

She wasn't dead, but she had double pneumonia brought on by complete exhaustion, Dr McLain said twenty minutes later. Everyone looked pale and anxious when the Ambulance men came and took her away on a stretcher. Grannie kept her arms round me all the time and I loved her, only it didn't help.

In that dark, lonely spare room where I'd been born, our safe, special Nursery world had come to an end.

PART FOUR

Nan was going to be ill for a long time, because even when she was ready to leave hospital, she had to have a long, long rest. Grannie kept me with her as much as possible, and the rest of the time Charlesworth and Maisie took turns to look after me. Being with Charlesworth was nicest of all. In her private pantry at the back of the basement, which looked out into a well between our house and the next so the sun could never quite get down there, she and Petty had a life of their own. The room was always dark and smelt of silver polish, dog and Lifebuoy soap, but I could hardly wait to run down there when Maisie and I came in from our walk.

Charlesworth would have tea ready on a card table Grannie had sent down specially and, with Petty in his basket on the floor between us, we shared our scones and sponge cake with him. Then, with a little soft brush I was allowed to brush the crumbs and butter off his beard while Charlesworth washed up. It was funny at first to think of Charlesworth having a family, but she had. They all lived in Ealing and she went there on her Sundays off. I thought the visits must be very sad because they all had Chronic Troubles, but when I said so Charlesworth sounded quite cross:

'Don't you go being so heartless, Miss Diana! We have a lovely time and there's no comfort like your own flesh and blood! They always has my old Gran's embroidered foot-stool put ready for me – shocking walk up from the station, it is – and my brother Ted – he works in a laundry – well, he takes the chance to rest his poor back on the sofa. Mind you, I'm not saying as how it doesn't get a bit warm in that sitting-room sometimes because his wife, Nell, has to keep a kettle steaming on the hob to ease her chest – wheezes like a cageful of sparrows, she does. 'Course, I'll admit the steam helps our Maisie as well, never did throw off her last heavy cold properly . . .'

Sometimes Charlesworth's sister came too, with her chilblains, but only if her husband's rheumatics weren't too painful for him to be left.

It sounded sadder than ever but I didn't say so. If one of them hadn't had a Trouble they might have felt lonely.

About a week after Nan went to hospital Charlesworth sent me up to the drawing-room for my half-hour with Grannie a bit early, because the pantry clock was fast. The door wasn't quite shut and I could hear Aunt Clare talking in a loud, angry voice, so I slipped inside and waited.

'It's time her own parents took charge of Diana.' Aunt Clare was striding up and down, looking at Grannie, so she didn't see me. 'Good God, Mother, haven't you done enough for the brat already? Let Georgina shoulder her own burden for a change and see how she likes it. I'll go to some agencies tomorrow and find a Nanny to take the child down to Devon. We can't do more.'

I crept out again and ran all the way upstairs to the Nursery. With Betsy Caroline I crawled under the big table and pulled the red cloth down on one side to make a sort of tent. I couldn't have a new Nanny when Nan was going to get better and come back. Besides, who would take care of our treasures if I went all the way to Devon? We'd looked it up on the map once, when I asked Nan if it was Foreign Parts, and it wasn't but it looked hundreds of miles away. I knew Mother's name was Georgina, of course, but I didn't understand how I could be her responsibility – and although I didn't know exactly what it meant, the way Aunt Clare had called me a 'burden' sounded horrid, especially if Mother had to carry it on her shoulders. She'd probably kick me away like the pink sugar mouse.

I began to cry and then made myself stop, holding Betsy

Caroline very, very close. If Aunt Clare came to look for me and found me crying, she'd send me to Devon even sooner, because when Nan was being taken away on the stretcher she'd said :

'For goodness' sake stop snivelling, Diana. It drives us all mad. Good heavens, you're six now, surely you can control yourself. Anyway, it's all your fault that Nan is ill. You and your endless illnesses and stupidity.'

Grannie was hugging me at the time and I hadn't really thought about it; Aunt Clare was always unkind. But now I did. Suppose Nan's illness *was* my fault? I hadn't meant to have measles and influenza or chicken-pox but . . . that last time, when we were in the spare room, was just that I was frightened of the Germans and I was too afraid to tell anybody, even Nan. Perhaps being sent to Devon was my punishment and if I was brave, like Jenny in the factory, then Nan might get better quickly . . .

A few days later Aunt Clare found Nurse McRawley. After Grannie and Grandpapa had talked to her in the drawing-room Aunt Clare brought her up to the Nursery.

Nan was very small and neat – not much bigger than me – but this woman filled our whole room. She was tall and fat with frizzy red hair and chins wobbling over the neck of her shiny blue dress.

'Come and kiss your new Nurse, Diana.' Aunt Clare's voice was creamy. 'Her name is Nurse McRawley and she's going to take you to live with Mother and Daddy the day after tomorrow. Won't that be lovely?'

'Yes.' I couldn't move. If I kissed that face I knew I'd be sick and Aunt Clare would be furious.

'Oh, well,' she said crossly, glaring at me, 'poor Nurse won't take long to find out how difficult you are. Perhaps you'll be more polite if I go.'

The minute she left the room Nurse McRawley snapped :

'Sit down! By the table. I want room to unpack.'

She lifted an old carpet bag on to the bed and I wondered how she could fit all her clean vests, knickers, nighties and dresses into anything so small. Nan and I needed a trunk and our two attaché cases whenever we went away.

She pulled out three wide belts made of red flannel, a grubby blue cardigan, a pair of slippers and a black brush and comb full of hair. Then she turned the bag upside down and an old pink dressing-gown fell out and that was all. She hadn't a pair of knickers or one single vest.

'Nosey, aren't we?' she said, pushing the empty bag under her bed. 'I'll be asking your Grandma about buying myself a uniform tomorrow.'

She marched out of the Nursery shutting the door behind her, and after she'd gone everything was so quiet I could hear ringing noises in my ears. I tip-toed over to my bed to fetch Betsy Caroline, terrified of making a sound. I thought it must be tea-time, but I wasn't sure because Nan had asked Charlesworth to take her little bedside clock to the hospital when she went on visiting day. I sat very still, hugging Betsy Caroline and whispering Nan's name over and over and over again although I knew it couldn't bring her back. *Surely* Grannie would send Nurse McRawley away if I explained that I was afraid to be alone with her and that she hadn't any knickers?

For the first time in my life I knew that this fear was real and not just imagination.

Dr McLain had told Grannie that she must stay in bed every morning until lunch-time, so the minute Nurse took our breakfast tray down to the kitchen next morning, I ran down and knocked on Grannie's door. She smiled and held out her hand when I went in, but Aunt Clare was sitting by the bed.

'What on earth are you doing here, Diana? You know Grannie has to rest.'

I'd been planning what to say ever since I woke up, but now the words wouldn't come. Instead I began to cry in great gulps which made it hard to talk at all.

'Please . . . please Grannie . . . send Nurse McRawley . . . away,' I managed. 'She – she only wears a red flannel thing . . . round her tummy . . . and I'm frightened . . .'

Aunt Clare came behind me, her hands on my shoulders,

and I knew Grannie thought she was being very kind and gentle, but she was gripping me so hard it hurt my bones.

'That's right, Clare,' Grannie said. 'Take the poor darling back upstairs. These turns are so bad for her . . . and things are bound to feel strange at first, Diana. It'll pass.'

Aunt Clare marched me back to the stairs and said: 'You selfish brat, upsetting Grannie like that. And if you were rude enough to watch poor Nurse undressing we shall be very lucky if she doesn't give notice at once.' She gave me a push. 'Get back to the Nursery and apologize to her the minute she comes up again.'

If only Grannie had been alone I could have explained that I wasn't being rude watching Nurse last night. She seemed to want me to, as she switched on the top light and banged about until, when she was all bare except for the flannel belt, she bent over my bed and pointed at Betsy Caroline.

'Take that nasty, smelly thing to bed, do you? Well, we'll see; I don't know how long I can put up with it in *my* nursery.' Nurse herself smelt horrible, hot and sour, so that I stuffed my hanky up my nose as soon as she turned the light off. Then I remembered that I might die if I didn't breathe, so I pulled it out again in case she threw Betsy Caroline away after I was dead.

Now, on my way upstairs, I realized that Betsy Caroline's face was wet with my tears and being wet always made her smell more of cork. I ran up the last stairs as quickly as I could to hide her before Nurse came. Nan and I had a special Treasure Box in the cupboard that held our knitting, a lovely pair of yellow wool plaits on a piece of elastic, and a china dog with a pink tongue that Nan's sister had won in a raffle. I tucked Betsy Caroline under all the knitting and asked God not to let Nurse McRawley find her until her face was dry. I tried not to ask for His help too often after pestering Him so much about my cork legs, but this was really important.

When Nurse came in, panting and red in the face, I knew it was going to be all right.

'Get your coat on, don't moon about. You're to come with me while I buy that uniform. Tho' how I'll manage on the money your Grandpa's given me I *don't* know.'

Betsy Caroline would be dry by the time we got back.

Daddy was at the small station in Devon to meet us. I was glad that he never tried to toss me up in the air any more but instead, on his rare visits to London, he'd bend down, peck me on the cheek and say: 'Being a good girl, Diana? That's right!'

It was the same at the station except that he added: 'Had a good journey, eh?' as the porter put my trunk and Nurse's two carpet bags (she'd bought an extra one for her uniform) into the boot of his touring car. Daddy lifted me on to the front seat beside him while Nurse, with a loud sniff, climbed in at the back. None of us said anything as we drove along, so it was more friendly when, after clearing his throat two or three times, Daddy started singing the Eton Boating Song in a loud, jolly voice.

I'd wondered a little on the train whether I'd ever be able to tell Mother and Daddy about Nurse McRawley but, seeing Daddy again, I knew that we should never talk any more than we'd done in London. Besides, if I started straight off being a Burden, like Aunt Clare said, Mother might send me away to live quite alone with Nurse.

'Here we are, then.' Daddy stopped singing and turned the car in through a white gate, driving up a stony drive with dark, shadowy trees on each side, and stopped in front of a long grey house covered with virginia creeper and squinting windows criss-crossed with black lines. He tooted the horn but nothing happened except that an old gardener came round the side of the house to help with the luggage.

'Ah, well, I expect Mother's resting,' Daddy said. I thought he sounded disappointed. 'Never mind, eh? I'll show you and Nurse to your quarters and then someone'll fetch you when Mother's ready.'

It was an unfriendly house, with narrow passages and steps going up and down as we walked on and on to the furthest end of it. Sometimes the light was green and dim where creepers grew right over a window. At last Daddy opened a door.

'Nursery Wing,' he said. 'Brought up my old school tuck-box specially for you to keep your toys in, Diana.'

'Thank you. I haven't brought any, actually, just Betsy Caroline's clothes.' It was true. I didn't want anything else to play with, but Daddy looked at me as if I'd said something odd.

'Oh – well – h'm – bedroom's next door, Nurse, bathroom etcetera just along the passage. Young Edna will bring up your tea in a few minutes, I expect.' And with a last startled look at me he left us alone.

'Nasty place, full of cobwebs,' McRawley grumbled as she went over to open a window. I liked it. There was no creeper here to turn the light green, and outside there was a yard where chickens scratched in the earth and clucked; beyond, there was a barn, very old and silvery with soft grey moss on the roof. When Nurse had gone next door to inspect the bedroom, Betsy Caroline and I leant on the windowsill and could just see a big garden to the left, full of apple trees and vegetables. When we could escape from Nurse it would be exciting to explore.

'Diana!'

I ran into the bedroom. She was standing at the top of one of the beds with a queer smile that frightened me, her eyes half shut.

'Open the window,' she said softly. 'Then come here – pick up that thing – and throw it out.'

The window was quite stiff and high up, and I wondered why she asked me to do it when she was much taller, but I managed. Then I went back and saw what she was pointing at. The old familiar churning began in my tummy and any minute I knew the flickering would start behind my eyes and I shouldn't be able to see properly. The thing was brown and furry, with black leathery bits on each side like wings, and stiff pink claws sticking up in the air. I knew it was dead though I'd only seen two dead things before, a sparrow in the gutter and a pigeon in the Park, but they'd had the same awful stillness which wasn't like being asleep at all.

'What is it?' I whispered. I was going to be sick and

turned to run to the lavatory, only Nurse caught my arm.

'It's a bat, that's what it is. I won't have nasty dead vermin in my room. *Pick it up.*'

I couldn't move and the room started swimming.

'If you don't do as I say *at once* I shall throw your dirty old doll away!'

I had to save Betsy Caroline, so I caught one of the leathery things between my thumb and finger and lifted it. The body sagged and icy claws scraped over my wrist. I ran to the window and flung it out. Then, shivering, I was very sick indeed.

'Disgusting child,' snorted Nurse McRawley. 'A maid'll have to clean that up, I'm certainly not going to,' and she pressed a bell as she went out of the room. I stayed where I was, crouched on the floor, still feeling those thin hard claws on my skin.

'There, there. Whatever is the matter, poor Miss Diana?'

The soft West Country voice was so kind I turned towards it and warm, plump arms went round me reassuringly. 'Now you leave everything to Edna,' the voice went on, 'and we'll have you washed and popped into bed in no time. No wonder you're a bit upset inside after that long journey.'

I couldn't tell her about the bat. I didn't think anyone would understand how dreadfully I'd minded if I said, 'I had to pick up a dead bat.' At least nobody except Nan, and Grannie had told me I must only send cheerful postcards to her while she was ill, and had given me some with stamps on to write every week.

Edna's face was just a blur because of the flickering, but her hands were gentle with a warm sponge and a soft towel. Then she put Betsy Caroline into my arms, tucked us into bed and I must have gone straight to sleep, because suddenly it was morning and I felt better.

When Edna came to clear away Nursery breakfast I saw that she was young and pretty with round blue eyes and a lovely smile. 'Your Mother'd like to see you now, Miss Diana,' she said. I liked her even more than when she had helped me yesterday, and took her hand so as not to get lost going through the house.

Mother was in bed looking beautiful in a mauve dressing-gown trimmed with lace frills, and her black hair, which I'd only seen coiled into a bun, was loose and thick round her shoulders. It was the prettiest room I'd ever seen, and I hoped she might let me look at the ornaments and bright necklaces spilling out of a box on the dressing-table beside a bowl of red roses.

'Aren't you going to come and kiss me, Diana?' she asked. I crossed the room gingerly, so afraid of bumping into anything that I accidentally stuck my tongue out – just once – because of trying so hard to be careful. Mother saw it and sighed.

'Oh, dear, haven't you grown out of that ghastly habit yet? I can't think why you do such *peculiar* things. You really must try not to when I have my friends here.'

She didn't mention kissing again so I stood stiffly by the bed, knowing that if I didn't keep quite still I was going to shrug my shoulder up, twitch my eyes and put my tongue out again – though I hadn't needed to do any of those things for a long time until that morning.

'I'm sorry you were sick last night,' Mother went on. 'I would have come up to see you only we had a dinner party, you see. Are you all right now?'

'Yes, Mother.' She sighed again.

'Well, run off to the Nursery, then. Daddy saw your nice Nurse yesterday evening and it's all arranged that she'll take you for a lovely walk every morning. Then you can play in the garden after lunch while she has a rest, and come down to the drawing-room for a little while at five o'clock, just like you did with Grannie.'

Only nothing here would ever be like it was in Grannie's house, and I trailed back along the endless passages with Edna. Suddenly she squeezed my hand.

'Cheer up, Johnny Bull,' she whispered. 'It's strange at first but you'll settle in nicely. You'll see.'

Nurse McRawley grumbled a lot under her breath while we got ready for that first morning walk, and she slipped a medicine bottle full of what looked like water into her big black bag before we started.

'Nosey,' she said crossly as I stared. 'Your poor old Nursie's got a bad heart and she didn't expect to be sent off on long walks. Has to be careful. Great nuisance it's only the beginning of the long school holidays, else you'd be kept busy all day there.'

We went out through a side door, round the house, and started down the drive towards the main gate. When we were under the dark trees and out of sight of the windows Nurse said:

'Off with your shoes and socks. Look sharp, now.'

'But I'm never allowed to take them off except at the seaside when there's sand and it's hot. Nan said I'd catch cold.'

'Well, your precious "Nan" isn't here now, is she? It's *my* say-so and I'm not polishing muddy shoes and washing socks every day so don't you think it. Take them off!'

I laid Betsy Caroline down on the leaves and did as I was told. 'What shall I do with them?' I asked her.

'What d'you suppose? Carry them, of course.'

It never occurred to me to run back to the house, to tell them about the bat and show them my shoes and socks. Nobody, except perhaps Edna, would believe me and Mother would only sigh some more and probably start talking French or German.

The flint stones hurt so much I could only hobble at first, clutching Betsy Caroline under one arm and the shoes and socks under the other. Nurse was far ahead of me, and when I got to the gate she was leaning against it drinking a dose of medicine out of her bottle. She looked at my feet, which were bleeding a little, and smiled the queer smile she'd had when she pointed to the bat.

'Soon toughen you up, little softie,' she said. 'Come on, Edna told me there's a golf course near here so you'll soon be walking on grass.'

There was, and the grass was cool and soft. I was glad because my feet didn't hurt quite so much and I was absolutely determined not to cry. I knew she wanted me to – like being sick the night before – but I wasn't going to do anything she expected ever again.

Only, the golf course had something else besides grass. After we'd walked a while Nurse needed another dose of medicine, and when she'd had it she shaded her eyes with a fat red hand, looking carefully over the smooth green space all round us. Suddenly she grunted and moved towards a blackish patch lying on the edge of some long grass. I tried hard to pray and even harder to think about Nan, but none of it would come – not through my painful feet and the awful feeling in my tummy. I knew what was lying there before we reached it.

The crow had been dead for a long time. There were crawling maggots instead of eyes and the feathers were stiff and hard. Black claws lay limp and flat against a rusty open patch that I couldn't look at.

'Pick it up, Diana. Pick it up and carry it over to those

bushes where it'll be out of sight. We can't have gentlemen finding a nasty thing like that when they're out golfing, can we?'

This time I wasn't just going to be sick, I was going to die. There was nothing left in the world except Jesus-Tender-Shepherd-Hear-Me and Betsy Caroline, and even they seemed unreal.

'Hurry up. Then we can stroll back to lunch.'

Lunch . . . First touching this terrible thing and then having to sit in front of slimy white fish and rice pudding. The prayers came then: 'Oh, Gentle Jesus – please *hurry* – take me to heaven now . . . Please . . .'

'Pick it up.'

I spread my socks carefully over Betsy Caroline's face so that she wouldn't see. I shut my eyes at first but then they flew open – suppose I touched the crow with my bare feet and the maggots crawled over them? Sick far beyond being sick, I picked the thing up and carried it to the bushes Nurse was pointing to. I knew that I'd feel those coarse, black feathers on my hands always, and I walked steadily back, picked up my shoes, socks and dear Betsy Caroline and said:

'You're wicked. I'm never, never going to speak to you again.'

She still had the queer smile. 'We'll see about that, my girl. Just you try it and you'll see! Your poor Mother thinks you're a bit touched and your Auntie's told her you're a liar, so don't go making up fancy tales because I can tell them some that might get you locked up for the rest of your life.'

I couldn't eat any lunch, even though it wasn't fish after all but brown chops with potatoes and brussels sprouts and a red jelly for pudding. All I could see on the plate was shabby black feathers. Nurse ate mine as well as all hers.

'No wonder she can't fancy her dinner,' said Edna, clearing away. 'Not after being sick last night. Never mind, Miss Diana, Cook's made you her special Gingerbread Monkeys for tea, you'll enjoy *them*.'

Directly Edna had gone Nurse, staggering a little, went

over to the big armchair and fell asleep, her mouth wide open and heavy snores making her chest shake. I crept out and went downstairs and into the garden. Nurse had made me put on my shoes and socks again before we got back to the house, and there were blood marks on them. If I could only find Daddy and show him – tell him about the bat and the crow, too – surely he'd understand? I needed to talk about it all now, to stop the crawling horror going round and round in my head.

He was chopping up a branch that had fallen off an oak tree by the stream that ran along the bottom of the garden. He looked nice with his shirt sleeves rolled up, and he seemed pleased to see me.

'Hello, Diana. Had a good walk this morning, eh?'

'No. It was beastly. Nurse told me to take off my shoes and socks so my feet are sore, and then she made me pick up a dead crow and hide it. It was full of crawling things.' I swallowed hard. Daddy roared with laughter.

'Bet you peeled off your own shoes and socks. I know I always did! Just don't try and pretend it was Nurse's doing, eh? And I'm glad to hear she's teaching you to be a country girl. Lived in London far too long – and good lord, this place is infested with crows – die all over the place. I chuck a couple over the hedge nearly every day and I'm glad you're getting the hang of it. Must learn not to be squeamish, y'know.'

So it was no use. Nurse was right and nobody was ever going to listen to me. I walked away, trying not to limp, and went right down among the gooseberry bushes at the end of the kitchen garden. A little nut-brown face popped up from behind one of them and said:

'Come looking for Devon pixies, have ye? 'Fraid there b'ain't none here but me, and I'm just picking gooseberries for Cook's pie.'

'I wasn't expecting pixies. It's only that my feet are very sore and I had to pick up a dead crow today,' I told him.

He came out on to the path with a bowl half full of gooseberries.

'Now that's bad,' he said. 'What ails your small feet?'

I hoped he wouldn't think me rude if I sat down while we talked, but my feet were throbbing and felt hot and sticky.

'I had to walk down the drive without my socks and shoes and the stones were awfully sharp.' He looked at my bloody socks and put down the bowl of gooseberries.

'I'll take ye in to Cook, Miss,' he said. 'Fair dab hand she is with her lotions and ointments, you'll see. Shall I carry ye?'

I got up painfully, and when we stood together he was only a little bigger than me so we both laughed.

'Mebbe we'll do better if I give ye me arm,' he said. So slowly, arm in arm, we went to the back door.

Cook was a big, fat, jolly woman covered from shoulders to feet in a huge white apron. She was rolling out pastry when we arrived, while Edna was sitting by the stove stirring something in a pan and reading aloud from a magazine at the same time. They were very surprised to see us.

'Just you look at they feet,' said the gardener. 'Bin made to walk barefoot on that wicked drive, she says.'

Cook peered down to look and it was difficult for her because her chest stuck out like a pillow. Then she made a clucking sound and shook her head.

'You sit down and get off those shoes, lovey,' she said. 'Couldn't understand why you didn't even peck at my lunch, even if you were bilious after your journey. But I see it all now. Get me a bowl of clean hot water, Edna,' she went on, 'and you get back to my gooseberries, Fellows, I'll be needing them in a jiffy.'

Sitting on a high-backed chair with the kindness of Cook and Edna all round me, I had the most wonderful idea. Surely Mother would send Nurse away if Cook told her about my feet and then I could come and live in the kitchen all the time and never bother Mother or Daddy again. Cook drew up a chair opposite me and began soaking my socks off so gently in the warm water that it hardly hurt at all. Edna was watching, her blue eyes like saucers, but I couldn't stop looking round the kitchen. It was such a glorious place my chest nearly burst with wanting to laugh and sing and shout all at once, it offered so many things to explore, so much to do if only Cook would let me help her. The long wooden dresser held shiny blue and white plates and, on top, rows of copper pans twinkled when I moved my head. Big stone crocks on the floor were labelled 'Flour', 'Sugar', 'Rice' and 'Oatmeal'. All the chairs and the big table were scrubbed white and a delicious smell of fresh baking was everywhere.

Cook's cooing and clucking turned into a sharp expression of horror when my socks were off at last.

'What really happened, Miss Diana?'

'Nurse McRawley made me take off my shoes and socks because she said she wouldn't clean and wash them every day.'

'H'm. Soon see about that, you poor mite.' She looked fierce, but it felt lovely when she put on some cool, white cream and then wrapped my feet in strips of clean soft linen. 'You need building up as well,' she added as she finished the bandaging. 'All eyes, skin and bone – we must get some good Devonshire cream and farm eggs into you. There, you sit quiet a bit and Edna will fetch you one of my Gingerbread Monkeys. *I'm* going up to see the Mistress.'

'Everything'll be all right now, Miss. Cook's got a grand way with her when she's set on something.' Edna was reaching down a pretty tin covered with flowers from a shelf. 'And in eight weeks or so school'll be starting up again. You'll like our school, Miss Diana, and make lots of friends. I only left for good a year ago and I was real happy there.'

She handed me a Gingerbread Monkey and he was so perfect I couldn't believe he was meant to be eaten. I wanted to keep him as a friend for Betsy Caroline to play with while I was asleep at night; it worried me that she couldn't go to sleep, ever, because her eyes wouldn't shut. How she'd love the Monkey! His round, brown face had black currant eyes and a big smile; his ears were round, too, and stuck straight out, but best of all he had a curly gingerbread tail curving up from the side of his tummy.

'Oh, Edna, I *couldn't* eat him – he's much too special.'

' 'Course you can, Miss. Cook's made a whole tinful just for your tea-times. They're like magic, Cook's Monkeys.'

Her rosy face glowed. 'When you eat one it makes you warm and happy inside. I know, because she made me a batch when I first come here to live in, and felt that homesick and mopey. But after a few Monkeys I felt ever so much better.'

'You're sure he's not the only one?' I longed to feel warm and happy inside – but I did want to keep him, too.

'Cross me heart. Look.' She held out the tin. 'All for you, these are.'

Very slowly, with Edna watching eagerly, I bit off an ear. It was the nicest thing I'd ever tasted and the Monkey went on smiling. I kept his face to the very last and Edna was right; the gingery taste *did* make you warm and happy inside.

Cook came back looking hot and flustered.

'Your Mother's gone to the Nursery to see that fine Nurse of yours, Miss, and she wants you to go straight up there as well. Careful now!'

I'd jumped down off the chair at once, frightened by her expression and forgetting my feet, which hurt again as they jolted on the floor.

'Is she very cross? I thought . . .'

What had I thought? That Mother might be so shocked she'd come down here to see me herself instead of believing I was a bit touched and a liar?

'You take another Gingerbread Monkey with you, lovey,' Cook pressed one into my hand and looked as if she was going to cry. 'Walk gently, now – and you come down here whenever you want. Me and Edna enjoy company.'

'Thank you. Thank you both very much. I do wish Nan was here, we'd all have lovely times together.' I hobbled out as quickly as possible because the picture of the four of us sitting round the big table playing Snap and eating Gingerbread Monkeys was so lovely I couldn't bear to be without Nan for another minute.

But I mustn't cry; it would make McRawley pleased, and even if Mother wanted to listen I shouldn't be able to say anything. Instead I hitched my shoulder and put my tongue in and out all the way upstairs. It didn't really help.

Mother was standing by the Nursery window dressed to go out to a tea-party, with her hair coiled on her neck under a wide leghorn hat decorated with lots of thin brown velvet ribbon. She was switching her beige kid gloves against the windowsill. Nurse, her face bright red, stood in front of the empty fireplace.

'Come in, Diana.' Mother's voice was annoyed and I felt the little Gingerbread Monkey crumble as I clenched him between my hands, waiting. 'You know, don't you, that you're a very tiresome, wicked child? Aunt Clare told me how troublesome you were in London, but I didn't believe you were a liar – until now. Imagine telling Cook all that nonsense about poor Nurse McRawley when you know you deliberately took off your shoes and socks after she'd forbidden it. She tells me you upset her so much she nearly came to me and gave notice! Well, what have you to say for yourself?'

I couldn't say anything. The distance between Mother and me was so great it could never be bridged by words. Just as she'd promised that morning, McRawley had won. Would always win.

'You punish her yourself, Nurse; I shall be out for tea and cocktails, but if you decide her father ought to smack her, perhaps you'll tell him? He's at home today.' Mother swept out, her coffee and cream silk dress rustling softly as she went. McRawley and I were alone.

I'd decided on my way upstairs that, if I was never going to speak to her again, I needn't call her 'Nurse' either, even in my mind. Nan once told me – when I'd read something by accident in her *Daily Mail* – that if you were a criminal and the police took you away, they only called you by your surname afterwards. And it was such an ugly surname, it suited her.

McRawley's voice was thick and red like her face. 'In the corner, Liar!' she said. 'I told you nobody would ever believe you, didn't I? No, not that corner, the one over there. Keep your head down and look at what's waiting for you.'

She must have put another bat there. I went over,

shutting my eyes tight. I still had the crumbs of a Monkey in both hands, though some of them dribbled down on to the floor.

When Edna brought tea in she must have looked at us both, but she scuttled out without saying anything except:

'Cook's sent you up something special, Miss.'

'Special!' McRawley's voice sounded a long way off. 'You'll not get anything special today, *miss* – telling dirty lies about me in the kitchen.'

She drank her tea noisily and I could hear her chewing; she never shut her mouth when it was full. I wondered if the Gingerbread Monkeys would make her feel cosy inside and I hoped they wouldn't.

Keeping my eyes so tightly shut made moons and stars dance behind my eyelids and they got fainter and fainter until I suddenly realized I was falling asleep. Asleep – with a dead bat on the floor! If I fell over I might hit it with my face, so I forced my eyes open though they felt stiff and heavy and my feet began to throb again.

Then the door opened and I heard Daddy say:

'Trouble up here, eh?' He didn't sound specially cross so I turned round quickly.

'She wants me to pick *that* up,' I said loudly. 'Like the other one, and the black crow . . .'

Daddy came over at once. Then he looked at me as if something odd was the matter.

'But there's nothing there, Diana. You're a rum little thing and no mistake, aren't you?'

He was right. There was nothing on the floor at all except a few crumbs. He went back to McRawley.

'From a note my wife left in the hall, I understand I might be needed for some spanking duty, Nurse. Is that so?'

'No, sir. She's stood in the corner long enough now.'

'Ah – good. Well – try not to keep imagining things, Diana, eh?' He seemed glad to leave us.

McRawley's eyes glinted. 'Well, that settles it, you nasty child. No one is *ever* going to believe you now, are they?'

We couldn't go for walks for a week because of my feet.

Mother sent some bandages and ointment up to the Nursery and said that, except on Nurse's afternoon off, I was not to go pestering Cook in the kitchen.

McRawley said she'd have to have some time off before long, and take a bus to the nearest town because her heart medicine was running short. One day, when she was asleep after lunch, I crept into the bedroom and opened the wardrobe carefully because it creaked after the first few inches. On the top shelf really meant for hats there were four empty bottles, and it seemed funny that anyone could drink so much medicine when it usually tasted so nasty. Was McRawley very, very ill, I wondered, perhaps ill enough to die? But if she was, then the doctor would keep coming and he hadn't been once yet. I got the wardrobe shut and ran over to my bed just as she woke herself up with a colossal snore that rattled. When she came in I was reading one of the letters I kept under my pillow.

Grannie wrote every week and there was always a pretty postcard from Nan on Mondays. Edna brought them up with our breakfast tray so McRawley couldn't stop me from reading them. Nan was coming out of the hospital soon and going to a nice quiet boarding-house on the front at Bognor with her sister, and she promised to look for lots of shells when she was stronger. The cards were in her lovely, round writing and were very precious because they meant she hadn't forgotten about me. That's why I kept them under the pillow, because McRawley made me make my own bed so I hoped they'd be safe there.

Grannie's letters were not very long and talked a lot about the weather. It seemed a dull sort of thing to go on about when I longed to know more exciting things, like whether Grannie's awful Street Singer still came round every Friday. She'd once sent him out a whole shilling when it was raining and after that he sang his song 'Oh, Where*ees* my boy tonight?' twice through for her each week. But it was seeing her handwriting, like Nan's, that really mattered.

I wrote back to them every Sunday, too. A letter to Grannie and a cheerful card to Nan, but as McRawley and Mother both read them before they were posted I couldn't say much. Mostly I told them how Betsy Caroline was and all about the Gingerbread Monkeys. Once I said that I'd found a beautiful little silky bird's nest in the kitchen garden with four blue eggs in it and was going to watch for the babies to hatch. But next time I went to look it had been destroyed and there were fragments of blue shell all over the ground.

It didn't matter how much McRawley slapped at me and shouted: I stuck to my promise never to speak to her again. It wasn't easy, as one long week followed another until it felt as if I'd been in that house forever. And on nearly every walk McRawley managed to find something dreadful for me to pick up. If there weren't any dead birds there was usually a mouse or a hedgehog that had been run over on the road, and they were almost worse because they were usually flat and messy, only at least they didn't have feathers. I couldn't forget the crow's feathers however hard I tried, and they were still there, sometimes, on my plate at meal-times so I couldn't eat the food.

But not speaking to her sometimes meant not speaking to anyone – except for saying 'Good morning' or 'Thank you' to Edna – for a whole week at a time. I wasn't sure what Daddy's work was, only that he was often away for several days. Most afternoons I saw Mother in the drawing-room for about twenty minutes, but she always had smart friends with her. They laughed all the time and smoked cigarettes in long black holders. Their lovely dresses and rows and rows of beads made me feel more ugly and awkward than ever in my serge skirt and blouse. My hair was straight, too, and often greasy, so that my ears stuck out because McRawley hated washing it and said that Nan's little rag curlers were 'a silly fiddle'. I didn't have a chance to speak in the drawing-room, either, because Mother answered for me if anyone asked a question.

So I began to worry about waking up one day to find I *couldn't* talk, like finding your legs too wobbly to walk on after being ill in bed for a long time. It was worse, really, than needing to put my tongue out, because I simply had to squeak every now and then to make sure my voice was still there. When I did it in the Nursery McRawley got terribly angry and slapped me, saying I was a raving little lunatic who ought to be shut up. I didn't mind her, but it was a pity when I squeaked in the drawing-room because Mother gave me one of her Long Looks and, after one of her friends said: 'Oh, poor Georgina, how *did* you produce It?' I wasn't allowed in the drawing-room for a long time.

In the end I solved it by talking out loud to Betsy Caroline in the kitchen garden every day. I explained it all to her first because we'd never needed out-loud words before. But she went on smiling so I knew it was all right, and she was pleased, too, because I'd managed to hide a Gingerbread Monkey after tea one day to be her friend. It was getting a bit difficult to keep him hidden in bed, actually, because without a tin to keep him fresh he was beginning to make a lot of crumbs, but I pushed them under my pillow among my letters and cards and promised Betsy Caroline I'd bring her a new one very soon; all the Monkeys looked exactly alike.

The leaves were turning yellow, and Edna had promised me that school would be starting in about a week, when McRawley said after breakfast one morning:

'Got a new walk for us today, *miss*. One you'll like, tho' you don't deserve it.' She had on her queer smile and my heart began thumping about as we went down the drive. What *could* be worse than the things she had made me do already? I moved Betsy Caroline up under my chin and put both arms round her.

We didn't go towards the golf course. Instead, we went down a pretty lane where there was a lovely, rushing sound as if both the bath taps had been turned on at once. We turned a corner and there it was – a river! It was wide and running very fast because a large waterfall close by was pouring down over mossy rocks like yards of shiny ribbon. I very nearly spoke to McRawley then, thinking she might have chosen this lovely place as a way of saying 'sorry' for all the dead things.

There wasn't time.

Before I realized, she was so close to us she snatched Betsy Caroline out of my arms and threw her – hard – right out into the water where it swirled away round a bend.

'*That'll* teach you to be a stupid, wilful girl, refusing to speak to your poor old Nursie and talking instead to that beastly, smelly bit of cork all day long! Oh, yes. I heard you through the window!'

I couldn't move, only stare and stare at the place where dear Betsy Caroline had disappeared. I heard the screams before I knew I was making them, and McRawley had become a hateful blue and red blur that I kicked and kicked and pummelled with my fists until she began screaming, too. Then she caught my wrists and started dragging me back to the house. She had to pull me along like a sack because I wouldn't walk.

I suppose Daddy must have heard the noise because he came to the front door to see what was going on. I wasn't screaming any longer, only sobbing Betsy Caroline's name.

'All this fuss,' I heard McRawley panting, 'just because her filthy old doll fell in the river. Smelly thing, it was, and full of germs, I'll be bound. I'd've asked Cook to burn it before long anyway.'

'Well,' said Daddy. 'Here's a fuss over an old doll! If you stop crying and don't disturb Mother, Diana, I'll bring you a splendid new one tomorrow when I go into town. Wouldn't you like a pretty, flaxen-haired china one in a pink dress, now?'

I shook my head, forced my wrists free, and ran and ran until I got to the gooseberry bushes. I threw myself down on the ground between them and cried until there were no tears left, only dreadful, gasping hiccups which hurt my chest. I couldn't get up and I never wanted to see anyone again, so at last I lay still, wishing I could die.

It was Edna who found me. She went down on her knees and cuddled me against her crackly apron. My eyes were too swollen to see her properly but she looked as if she was going to cry too.

'Oh, you poor one, you poor mite, *she* threw your doll

away, didn't she?'

I mumbled: 'Betsy Caroline was *real*.'

'Of *course* she was, anybody could tell that.' She was rocking me gently to and fro, making the soft clucking noises that had comforted me on my first night here. My eyes felt so heavy and sore it was lovely to shut them and feel safe.

I don't remember being carried into the house, but I must have slept all through the rest of the day because when I opened my eyes I was in my bed and it was nearly dark. I reached for Betsy Caroline before I remembered what had happened. Then I looked cautiously over the edge of the bedclothes. McRawley was sitting on the edge of her bed all bare except for her red body belt, taking her heart medicine by tipping the bottle into her mouth. She must have had the afternoon off to go and buy some more.

I hated her so much that I was glad she was so ugly, and I hoped I'd hurt her when I kicked her legs and hit her. Thinking of Betsy Caroline I felt as though something had broken into little pieces inside me and the pieces wouldn't come together again. Careful not to make a sound, I reached under the pillow to feel Nan's postcards. They'd gone. So had Grannie's letters. All that was left were a few crumbs from the Gingerbread Monkey.

Next day I had a temperature so Mother sent for the doctor and McRawley sat in a chair with her legs wide apart reading a newspaper for most of the time. The doctor was a tall, greyish man with the same soft voice as Cook and Edna, but I couldn't answer many of his questions because Mother and McRawley were there all the time. All the same I was glad he looked at my feet after he'd listened to my chest, and the way he said 'H'm' made me wonder if he had guessed what really happened. The cuts had healed but there were still red marks and bumps.

He looked at me, then at Mother and McRawley, before he wrote a prescription.

'Keep her in bed,' he said. 'There must be no excitement and she's to take this mixture three times a day after meals – light meals, mind. Eh, it seems a shame to keep Nurse cooped up in here all the time. Have you a girl in the household who could relieve her a bit?'

'Yes,' Mother sounded surprised. 'I daresay Edna might sit with Diana in the afternoons.'

'Good. Fine. I'll look in the day after tomorrow.'

Each morning I pretended to go to sleep again the moment I'd had my breakfast egg, milk, and the medicine which tasted of peppermints-a-long-way-off. Sometimes I really did sleep and that was lovely because it brought the afternoon time with Edna more quickly. We knew that McRawley would be safely snoring away in the day nursery, so when I told Edna I loved stories, she smuggled up some of the magazines she read aloud to Cook. Lots of them were just like Jenny and Mr Anstruther in the factory, and we both got very excited when we knew the happy ending was coming.

We were so enthralled on the third afternoon that we didn't hear the doctor come into the room until he clapped, which startled us both. Edna jumped up and hid the magazine under her apron, her face very pink.

'No need to do that, my dear,' he said, smiling. 'I think this is the best medicine Miss Diana could have.' His face stopped smiling. 'I just looked in on the day nursery and found Nurse sleeping well. You go and fetch tea now,' he told Edna. 'Miss Diana's mother is out and don't you disturb Nurse whatever you do.'

Edna crept out quietly and the doctor sat on the end of my bed. 'Now, young lady, d'you feel like telling me what all this is really about? You're not ill, you see, and I'm thinking I might be able to help . . . How about it?'

Hugging my knees, I began. I told him every single thing, starting with Nan being taken ill, and he never interrupted once. At the end I was crying but all he said was:

'Don't cry, Diana. I want you to give me your Grannie's name and address and I'll not get it down properly if you start hiccups!'

'You mean you'll write to her? Tell her truly about McRawley and my feet and the dead birds and everything? I can't myself because Mother reads the letters and she and Daddy don't believe me.'

'I know. I've had quite a talk with them.' His voice sounded cool but his eyes were still kind. 'You're a lonely, imaginative little creature, aren't you? And I daresay you exaggerate a bit, but – you give me that address and leave everything to me, eh?'

I gave it eagerly, making sure he'd got it absolutely right. 'Do you think Grannie and Nan might come and see me? Nan's feeling much better now, she said so on her last card . . . in fact she may go back to Grannie's soon.'

'We'll see, we'll see. Meantime, not a word to anyone. Don't you think that's best?'

'Oh yes, I do. *Honestly*, I'm not telling lies.'

'H'm,' he said, but it didn't sound at all like the puzzled way Daddy said it. 'You enjoy your tea, now – and don't fret. I'll be keeping an eye on you.'

He got up, and as he went to the door he opened the wardrobe and looked at the top shelf. Then he said: 'H'm!' again as he went out.

I was allowed up the next day, but for a week I was only to play in the garden and not go for walks. I was glad not only because of McRawley and the dead things but because I seemed to have grown a lot and my shoes hurt. They pinched and squeezed, but I didn't tell Mother because I'd heard her telling Daddy not to squander money on a new doll for me as they couldn't afford it and I knew shoes were expensive. Nan used to pay several pound notes each time we went to Daniel Neal to buy new pairs.

On the seventh evening, while I was eating my supper in the Nursery, McRawley said:

'Got a nice surprise for you, Diana. Not that you deserve it, mind! I expect you miss your old dolly in bed, though, so there's a little present waiting for you instead.'

I felt excited. She'd been on the bus to fetch some more heart medicine, and I thought she might be really sorry this time, and perhaps she'd bought me another cork doll or even one of the tiny sixpenny Teddy-bears from Woolworth's that Nan and I had planned to buy just before we were both ill.

While I gulped down the last two spoonfuls of junket I heard a car, very faintly, in the drive. It must be Daddy coming home, but he wouldn't come up to the Nursery as late as this. In fact he didn't usually come at all. I got off my chair.

'Can I look now, please?' I'd forgotten about not speaking to her and her smile wasn't in the least queer as she said: 'Clean your teeth first, remember. Nice surprises aren't for dirty little girls.'

I brushed and rinsed them twice to make sure it was *really* going to be a nice surprise. I missed Betsy Caroline more and more and, though nothing could ever take her place, it would be friendly to have something in bed with me. I'd tried taking a Gingerbread Monkey but in the morning he was nothing but a lot of crumbs and two currants which had stuck to my cheek.

'I've done my teeth twice, Nurse – may I go and see now?'

She was still sitting in the Nursery taking some heart medicine.

'Yes. I've hidden it a bit for fun, so you take off your dressing-gown, hop into bed and stretch your legs down till you find it.'

I stood by the bed for a little while wondering what it could be. There didn't seem to be a hump anywhere, so perhaps it *was* a little Teddy-bear from Woolworth's – and it would be cheating to look.

I laid my dressing-gown on the chair, then jumped into bed, shut my eyes and reached carefully down with my feet.

Next minute I was huddled up on the pillow screaming: 'Help – help – oh, please somebody come . . . *It's a dead bird* . . .'

The door opened and there, of all people, stood darling Grandpapa peering at me over his half-moon spectacles. I flew straight across the room and into his arms, so terrified I didn't even wonder how he'd got here.

'It's dead – in my bed,' I kept sobbing over and over again.

Holding me in his arms, my head buried against his shoulder, Grandpapa went over to look, pulling the bedclothes right back. Then he carried me straight out of the room and along several passages.

'Now, Diana darling,' he said gently. 'This is my room. Do you understand?' I nodded against his coat. 'I'm going to have to leave you here for a little while because I have things to see to, but I shall lock the door behind me so that no one – *no one* – can possibly come in. Will you be all right?'

'Yes, Grandpapa. I promise.'

'Good. You won't have to wait very long because I'm going to take you home to London with me on the late night train, but I must see your mother first and arrange to have your things packed. Grannie and Nan will both be there to welcome you when we arrive in the morning.'

He laid me on the bed and pulled the eiderdown round me before he went out, leaving all the lights on. It was a musty, comfortable room full of old, dark furniture, but even there I crouched right up on the pillow with my legs tucked under me. I pulled the eiderdown round my shoulders and curled the end tightly round my feet, still feeling the stiff feathers and cold little claws touching them.

It was to be twenty years before I dared to stretch my legs out in a bed again.

PART FIVE

Just as Grandpapa had promised, Grannie and Nan were in the hall waiting for us. It was wonderful to be back in the dear, familiar house in London, but for a moment I wanted to run away – the two people I loved most in the world had changed so much. Grannie, who had been so tall and straight, stooped now and I could see all the bones in her face. And Nan! During her illness they'd cut off her beautiful plaits and her short hair had turned white. I hugged Grannie first, so as not to hurt her feelings, because hugging Nan would prove that I was really home again. Then I buried my face against her grey cardigan and the lovely, Nursery smell of lavender bags and Mennen's talc powder hadn't changed a bit.

We all helped Grannie up to her bedroom. She had come down specially to welcome me because usually, Nan whispered, she spent all day in bed now. Then, at last, we went up the Nursery stairs.

'Oh, Nan!' There was such a big lump in my throat I could only croak. It was so perfectly, beautifully the same. Then I noticed the difference. There was only one bed there.

'Don't worry, darling.' Nan put her arm round me. 'I'm just next door in the old box-room. Grannie's had it made into a dear little bedroom, and if you just tap on the wall I shall hear. Come and see it.'

It was pretty but I hated it. I couldn't bear Nan not to be with me. She drew me down on to the bed beside her, holding my hand.

'You've grown a lot, Diana, in these months, and things

have changed here, too. You see, I have to look after Grannie now, almost as much as you, and there's a bell here by my bed in case she needs me in the night. We didn't want you to be woken up all the time. But let's go back to the Nursery now, I've got a surprise for you!'

On my bed was a parcel done up in tissue paper – and a shoe-box.

'Which shall I open first?'

'The parcel,' said Nan. 'You may not want what's in the box now you're older, it was only an idea I had.'

Inside the parcel were four of the little Teddy-bears from Woolworth's, and Nan had given each of them a different coloured bow.

But the shoe-box held a miracle; Nan's two plaits, tied with blue ribbon. They made everything right again and I took the shoe-box to bed with me every night until I had to go away to boarding-school.

I hugged her very, very hard and said: 'I wish I had a present for you, only we never went to the shops, only to . . .' I couldn't bear to think about the golf course or the river, it made them so real. Nan must have known because she said:

'Don't talk about it, darling, not yet. Let's get your unpacking done and then Grannie says we can go round to the Grocer and Mr Maloney's as a special treat this morning, because all you'll want after lunch is a good long sleep after that journey. I'll stay here with you, don't worry,' she went on, 'I'll have my rest in the rocking-chair and cast on for your new school jersey.'

I was to have breakfast and lunch in the dining-room to save Nan carrying heavy trays upstairs, so tea was our only private time when we could really talk. Aunt Clare had tea with Grannie and read the Bible to her. Nan told me Aunt Clare was thinking of Entering the Roman Catholic Church. She went to Mass every morning and spent hours in the dining-room being 'prepared' by someone called Father Stephen who lived in a thin, grey house sandwiched between our Greengrocer's and his church.

It took a week before I was able to tell Nan all about

Devon and McRawley. I was too big and heavy to sit on her knee any more, so I sat on the floor by her chair and she stroked my hair. At the end she said:

'She was a very, very wicked woman, darling. But you're safe and sound now, and you must try hard to forget all about it.'

But the very next day when Maisie and I went for our afternoon walk so that Nan could rest, I thought I saw McRawley in the street.

'Take me home, take me *home*,' I shouted, tugging at Maisie's hand, and she went pink because people passing turned to stare. We were running by the time we got to the Square, and I ran up all the stairs to the Nursery forgetting that I might disturb Nan.

'Whatever's the matter, Diana?' she asked. 'Not ill, are you?'

'I saw her. *I saw McRawley near the Park.*' I clung to the table. 'I'm never going out of the house again, Nan, not even to go to school next week.'

That evening when he came in, Grandpapa sent for me. We sat side by side on the drawing-room sofa and he said:

'It's a shame that you had a fright this afternoon, Diana; we all know what a difficult time you've had, you know, and we're so sorry. Mother and Daddy are very sorry now, too. But you must forget Nurse McRawley altogether, do you understand?' That's what Nan had said, but neither of them understood. McRawley might come any time, if we weren't in the Nursery, and put a dead bird in my bed.

They didn't know about her queer smile and slitty eyes that meant she'd found one. Grandpapa went on:

'Will you trust me when I tell you that Nurse McRawley has been shut up in a special hospital that she can never leave? It's called being certified. And she can never leave, as long as she lives.'

'But she wasn't ill, Grandpapa, was she?'

'She was very seriously ill, Diana. And I promise that there is no chance of you ever seeing her again. So now will you let Maisie take you out in the afternoons and take you to school?'

I looked up at him for a long time before I finally nodded. Then he lifted his veined hand with the heavy signet ring on the little finger and touched my face: 'Poor darling,' he said.

I felt much better when I went upstairs again. I hoped Nan would explain about McRawley's special hospital, but she didn't; only kissed me and said I must believe Grandpapa because what he'd told me was true.

It was nice being back at school again every morning. Huberta Watson-Leigh had left and gone away to a boarding-school, but Deborah was still there. I didn't tell her anything about Devon, I didn't think I would tell anyone, ever.

But at home Aunt Clare had 'got religion' as Nan called it, quite badly. It even made her look different. Instead of pretty, short frocks she had a long grey skirt and jacket for weekdays and the same in black for Sunday. With both she wore plain white shirt blouses and a floppy grey straw hat that bounced up and down when she walked, only just missing her nose. Nan said she'd packed all her frocks and beads away in a trunk.

I was pleased that she used her creamy voice all the time, though, and didn't get cross with me, so when she asked if I'd like to visit her new church with her I said I would. Aunt Clare carried a big prayer book printed in Latin and looked very holy while we walked along – though it was only a Wednesday afternoon – and she didn't talk at all. As we passed the Greengrocer, Joe, the delivery boy who was Walking Out with Maisie now, waved to me but I just flapped my hand behind my back, hoping he'd see, in case a real wave disturbed Aunt Clare's churchiness.

Inside St Michael's it was dark and musty at first, and when Aunt Clare stopped suddenly, dipping her hand into a little shell of water and curtseying right down to the ground, I nearly fell over her. Then she pushed open a heavy, brown baize door and said in her deepest voice: 'Welcome, little sister. Welcome to the One True Church.'

I hoped nobody was listening because it made me feel shy, but once we were properly inside I thought the Church was simply beautiful. There were rows of lighted candles all over the place, mostly in front of small, brightly-painted statues. The musty smell was stronger but I was beginning to like it.

A tall man in a long black dress with a tea-cosy on his head came out of the shadows. He had squeaky shoes which reminded me of Charlesworth's new pair that she said hurt her something chronic.

'Father Stephen,' throbbed Aunt Clare, 'I've brought this new Lamb, my niece, Diana. I know she will come to See The Light as I have.'

'Hello, Diana.' He shook my hand and smiled. His eyes twinkled as if we shared a funny secret so I stopped feeling shy about Aunt Clare. Father Stephen was obviously used to her. 'While your Aunt makes her confession I expect you'd like to look round?'

'Only don't touch anything!' Aunt Clare said in her old, 'how dare you' voice.

'Of course I won't.' As if I'd touch anything in a church!

She and Father Stephen disappeared into a little cupboard against the wall, though they each went in through purple curtains at opposite ends. I wondered how Aunt Clare would find room to make anything in there but I didn't worry about it because I wanted to look at all the statues. Most of them were Mary in a long blue dress holding the baby Jesus and they all had golden haloes. She didn't cuddle Him very well; every one of the babies had its arms out and was kicking, and her hands hardly seemed to be holding on to Him at all. But there was one lovely statue of Jesus as a man: His dress was brown and He was holding out His hands while the candles burning in front of Him made His face flicker as if it was smiling. I smiled back and then I noticed a bundle of white candles and a box of matches lying on a black tin box. Across the top it said: 'For the Dear Departed.'

I longed to light one and stick it in one of the empty holders, but the only Dear Departed I knew was Betsy Caroline and I wondered if Jesus would mind her being a doll or not? I didn't like to ask Him out loud in case Aunt Clare heard me, but I watched him carefully and we went on smiling at each other so I felt sure it was all right. I balanced the candle in the holder before striking a match. It burned more brightly than all the others at first; and then, putting the matches back, I saw another notice lower down on the box, above a little slit: 'Price for One Candle 1d. Please Insert Here.'

I hadn't brought any money, so I'd stolen it, and I'd *have* to tell Aunt Clare. I crept away and curled up on a slippery pew near her cupboard, wondering what punishment could ever be bad enough for stealing in church. If she had me sent to prison, no one would ever call me 'Diana' again, just my surname like the other criminals. As soon as she and Father Stephen came out of their cupboard I stood up quickly, wanting to get it over:

'I'mverysorryI'vebeenwicked. IlitacandleforBetsyCaroline beforeIsawtheycostapenny. Please – I didn't mean to steal it.' The words stopped bumping into each other by the end and at least I'd got it all out in one breath.

'Diana! You wicked, blasphemous little thing, lighting a candle for a *doll*! I'll put the penny in and then speak to you very seriously indeed when we get home. Which box was it?'

But Father Stephen had pulled up one side of his long dress showing ordinary black trousers underneath, and he handed me a penny from his pocket.

'It certainly isn't blasphemy. I'm sure Diana loved her doll very much. Here you are, Diana, go and put the penny in yourself. That'll make everything all right.'

Aunt Clare went off religion soon after that because Great-Uncle Patrick wrote to Grannie from Brighton, where he and Great-Aunt Madge were having a holiday, to ask if Aunt Clare would like to go back to Hong-Kong with them for a long visit.

Everybody thought it was a splendid idea, so Nan had to spend nearly all day unpacking and ironing Aunt Clare's smart clothes again. She bought a lot of new thin dresses, too, because Great-Aunt Madge sent a postcard of Brighton Pier to tell her it would be very hot Out East.

While Nan was busy ironing in the linen room I found some more coupons for free samples in the newspaper. I could only afford one stamp that week, though, because I'd spent 2d on a bag of hundreds and thousands, so I had to choose carefully. In the end I decided on a baby food because there was a picture of it saying 'Actual Size' and it looked such a dear little tin.

Nan was too flustered to look at the envelope and Maisie didn't bother; she was pleased to go to the Post Office instead of the Park that afternoon as it meant passing the Greengrocer and she might see Joe for a few minutes.

Our house was fairly quiet at that time because most of the Great-Aunts and Uncles were away. They liked having holidays in the autumn, Nan said, because places weren't so crowded. Only Great-Aunt Gussie never went away at all because she preferred playing Bridge every afternoon at her Club. When I discovered that Bridge was just a card game I thought she was silly; even Snap would get dull if one played it all the time.

The day Maisie and I posted the coupon Nan warned me to be extra good when I went down to the drawing-room after tea.

'Your Great-Aunt Gussie's there and in a fine old temper. They've closed her Club for a week to do up the rooms. So whatever you do, don't upset her, will you?'

The rules didn't seem quite fair. Nobody ever told Great-Aunt Gussie not to upset *me* and she still thought that calling me Skinny Lizzie and prodding my bony knees was very funny. She even screwed in her monocle to have a better look. Nan said I mustn't mind because it was much better to be thin and able to run and jump about, than be fat and get out of breath after climbing one flight of stairs like Great-Aunt Gussie.

But when I went into the drawing-room that afternoon Grannie was holding a letter that had come by the four o'clock post and she was saying to Great-Aunt Gussie:

'My dear, what are we to do? Matthew won't like it at all. He never cared for Vincent, anyway, and after that dreadful scandal when Father packed him off to Australia I never dreamed he'd come back, did you?'

'Don't be stupid, Elizabeth. That was thirty-odd years ago. Far as I can make out, Vin has lived amongst twenty thousand sheep ever since and if *that* hasn't drummed all the rakish ideas out of him, nothing will.'

Then they both saw me, and Grannie folded the letter away quickly into her handbag that went everywhere with her.

'Hello, darling,' she said, trying not to sound flustered. 'I didn't see you there. Come in.'

'Skinny as ever, I see,' Great-Aunt Gussie boomed, but she didn't poke me or put in her monocle and I got the feeling that the letter from this Vincent person had put her in a very cheerful mood. I could hardly wait to ask Nan who he was and what he'd done to be packed off to Australia. It sounded as if Great-Grandfather had had him done up in a parcel but I didn't think it could be that.

And I could tell the letter had upset Grannie. She looked paler than ever, and her hand shook a little as I went to her chair and she lifted it to stroke my hair as she always did. But Great-Aunt Gussie never bothered about other people's feelings.

'You're going to meet a new Great-Uncle soon, Diana, Grannie's and my brother, Vincent. Coming all the way from Australia.'

Grannie looked at me, and I realized for the first time that we could talk without words just like Nan and I had to do sometimes.

'Would you mind going back to the Nursery, darling?' she asked. 'Come and see me in my bedroom later. I'll be going up soon, will you tell Nan?'

I kissed her and ran. Nan was so surprised to see me she dropped a stitch, but when I told her: 'A new Great-Uncle called Vincent is coming from Australia – and he did something awful. Do you know what it was? It was bad enough for Great-Grandfather to send him there thirty years ago like a parcel. But Great-Aunt Gussie is pleased he's coming and Grannie is very upset.'

Nan looked worried. 'No, darling, I'm not sure what he did, it was before my time. But if Grannie's upset had I better go down?'

The house was so full of whispers and secrets about Great-Uncle Vincent that I'd forgotten about my sample tin of baby food by the time it arrived. I'd forgotten to warn Charlesworth, too, so I first saw the small, round packet on her silver tray when she carried the post to Grandpapa after Prayers. I ran to his chair.

'Please, Grandpapa, I think that's for me. May I have it?'

Grandpapa peered at it over his gold half-spectacles and Aunt Clare looked over his shoulder, hoping for another postcard from Great-Aunt Madge about Hong-Kong. Suddenly she snatched up my parcel, flung her hand out dramatically as she'd done as Britannia in the Parish Concert, then held it under Grandpapa's nose.

'My God, *look*!' she said in her fiercest voice. 'Something will have to be done about this child before I go away. She can't be trusted for a minute.'

Grandpapa slowly read out the coupon I'd filled in, which they always stuck on top of the packets like a label. He read my name – with 'Miss' printed after it in brackets – followed by our address. Then he stopped and his white moustache quivered as if he was laughing. He went on reading aloud:

' "When is the baby expected?" ' He looked at me over his glasses, sounding surprised and pleased I thought. 'I see from your answer that you seem to be expecting one in May, Diana.'

'It's such a warm month,' I explained. 'The baby wouldn't get cold waiting for me to find it if it was out of doors.'

Aunt Clare snatched the packet out of his hand.

'*Disgraceful!* A thing like that sent here, to this house, and addressed to an unmarried girl! If I'm to be in Hong-Kong for some time then surely, if only for Mother's sake, Diana ought to be sent to boarding-school. She'll soon be seven now and more impossible to control than ever!'

She threw my parcel into the wastepaper basket.

Nan and I puzzled a lot over why sending for baby food was so disgraceful.

'Though it was me not being married that made Aunt Clare so cross,' I remembered. 'Do you think babies aren't just found, Nan? Are they a secret people are only told about after a wedding?'

Nan went rather pink. 'Oh, Diana, you'd have to ask Grannie a question like that. Not being married myself, I'm not absolutely sure.'

It was three days before Grannie was strong enough to go down to the drawing-room so that I could ask her; she sometimes spent nearly a week in bed now. Aunt Clare had forgotten to be cross with me, too. She'd been round to see Mrs Watson-Leigh and asked all about the boarding-school where Deborah was going next term. It was called 'Glen Coe' and was by the sea, and Grandpapa had written to ask for something called a Prospectus.

It was so lovely to see Grannie sitting in her big chair again, and smiling, that I hugged her and then asked, very quickly in case she started talking about school:

'Please Grannie, where do babies come from? Really, I mean. And is it very important for people to be married first?'

'Darling! What a question! You don't need to worry your head about babies for several years yet.'

Aunt Clare came in while she was saying that, and she surprised us both by saying:

'This is the nineteen twenties, Mother – Victorian prudery

is hopelessly out of date. When a child asks questions nowadays they must be answered honestly. *I'll* tell Diana all she wants to know. Come to my room, Scrap.'

I didn't see how she could know much about it, not having been married yet and, following her upstairs, I wasn't sure that I wanted to know any more. At least, not from her.

Her room smelt of heavy, musky scent, and whenever she talked seriously to me we sat side by side on her bed so we both got covered with green, yellow and violet patterns from a stained-glass picture she'd hung against the middle of her window when she was having religion.

'Now, Little Fellow,' she began. My toes curled under inside my new, bigger shoes. She was going more and more throbby and I wished she'd just use my name. 'Babies!' She breathed heavily and I stared at the floor. Then she started again and I thought she'd changed her mind and was talking about something else:

'You've been in the country, and the Park. Haven't you sometimes watched the bees?'

'They fly about,' I mumbled.

'Ah, but surely you've seen a bee collecting pollen from one flower and taking it to another?'

'I don't think so. When a bee comes near I always run away. Nan's sister was stung by one once and her whole arm swelled up like a purple balloon.'

Aunt Clare stopped throbbing and sounded cross.

'Not being very helpful, are you? I'm beginning to think Grannie's right and you *are* too young for such things. However, as I'm going to Hong-Kong next month and you'll be off to boarding-school just after Christmas before I get back, perhaps the best thing will be for me to give you a very important and beautiful thought to carry with you – then you can never go wrong. Always remember, Scrap, that, inside, your body is a Temple. It is as sacred as the most holy church.'

'You mean full of little statues and candles like St Michael's?' I looked at her patterned face and forgot all about babies. The idea was tremendously exciting and I sat up very straight. It would be terrible if I slumped down or even jumped about any more, all my lovely statues and candles would bump into each other, and if they toppled over how could I pick them up if they were inside me? I carefully edged off the bed without bending anything. I could hardly wait to tell Nan.

'You won't forget, Little Fellow, will you?'

'Never, Aunt Clare,' I promised fervently. 'Thank you.'

Nan wasn't as excited as I expected. All she said was: 'That Aunt Clare of yours!' Then she looked at me anxiously. 'Why are you standing stiffly like that? This isn't going to start you off on another of Your Habits, is it?'

'No. But I don't want them all to fall over.'

Nan thought for a minute and then she had a wonderful idea. 'If what your Aunt says is true, then surely you've had those statues inside you ever since you were born! They haven't worried you yet, so why think about them now?'

The prospectus from 'Glen Coe' and another letter from Great-Uncle Vincent arrived at the same time. Grannie stayed in bed all that day and Grandpapa only ate half his eggs and bacon at breakfast. Then, as he pushed back his chair, he remembered I was there and pushed the prospectus towards me.

'Looks a very pretty place,' he said. 'See if you like the sound of it.'

'Surely you're not asking the opinion of a child of *six*?' Aunt Clare protested. Some of the new clothes she had bought were rather tight so she was on a diet, and dry toast and black coffee made her very bad-tempered at breakfast.

'Why not?' Grandpapa hardly ever looked cross but he did then. 'You weren't much of a judge, were you, Clare? Diana may as well get some idea of where she's going this time.' He went out. I knew he'd been thinking of McRawley and so did Aunt Clare. She went very red and put a big spoonful of marmalade on her last bit of toast. I snatched up the prospectus and went to get ready for school. Maisie walked me there now, but Nan was always in the hall with my hat, coat and satchel. I gave her the precious booklet.

'You read it first,' I said as I struggled into my coat. It was getting small but we'd agreed to make it do as I should have to have a whole new uniform for boarding-school. 'The picture on the front is lovely.'

We pored over it at tea-time. At least we took it in turns to pore because Nan was only really interested in lists like 'Black stockings, 6 prs. Navy knickers, 6 prs.' while I wanted to read about the classes and games, games like hockey and netball which I'd never heard of.

I took the prospectus down when I went to see Grannie in her bedroom, and asked her about them.

'Oh, netball is *very* nice, darling. You throw a large ball into a network basket and you should be very good as you're getting tall. But I don't think we should let you play hockey, it can be very dangerous.'

'*Dangerous?*'

'Yes. It's played with hard sticks and often the girls hit each other. Your grown-up cousin Esther still has a nasty scar on her chin, it quite spoils her looks.'

I began to wonder if boarding-school was going to be so nice after all. But I wasn't asked any more. A week later Grandpapa told Nan it was all arranged for me to start in January so we'd better go to Gorringes one afternoon and order my uniform.

In the meantime all the Great-Aunts and Uncles were coming back to London. The first Sunday they all came to lunch again (except dear Great-Aunt Felicity and her husband who had gone back to India), Grannie came down specially and I sat beside her. I kept so quiet they soon forgot I was there. Great-Aunt Madge looked quite different; she'd got a new, short wig with a fringe and it was bright yellow, but she laughed as much as ever and told Aunt Clare to be sure and buy a tin trunk or all her pretty clothes would be eaten by insects.

Aunt Clare went white and said: 'Not *spiders?*'

'Lor' bless you, yes – all over the place. Big ones, too, but you'll soon get used to 'em,' chuckled Great-Aunt Madge.

'But it's the ants that get among your clothes. You won't worry after a bit – we never do.'

I felt sorry for Aunt Clare. She minded spiders as much as I minded dead birds, but it was too late to change her mind. Grandpapa had bought her ticket from Thomas Cook's and they were all sailing in a week's time. She stayed very quiet all through lunch, but nobody noticed because, forgetting me, Great-Aunt Gussie began talking about Great-Uncle Vincent.

'Pity you'll miss seeing Vin,' she said loudly. 'Glad you're going to let him stay here after all, Matthew; but with Clare gone and that young maid of yours engaged to the Green-grocer you'll have nothing to worry about.'

Grandpapa looked at her over his spectacles. 'My dear Gussie, Vincent must be nearly sixty now, he's hardly likely to chase young girls at his age!'

Aunt Madge burst out laughing so that all her beads danced and jangled. 'Don't you believe it – some get worse as they get older!' She nudged Great-Uncle Joe on her left which set him off blinking his eyes faster than ever, and Great-Aunt Alicia said:

'Really, Madge! What you're sayin' is in extremely bad taste.'

'Sorry, I'm sure!' Great-Aunt Madge put on a funny voice but I knew she still thought it was very amusing, though she didn't say any more after Great-Uncle Patrick bent over and whispered something to her.

When I got upstairs I asked Nan: 'Do you suppose Great Uncle Vincent still chases young girls? Everyone in the dining-room seemed to think it was a wicked thing to do – except Great-Aunt Madge – but why? I think it would be lovely to have a Great-Uncle who chased me over the house, we could play hide-and-seek!'

Nan looked worried. 'I don't think they mean that kind of chasing, darling. But you needn't worry, he'll be an elderly gentleman now and besides you're his great-niece.'

'What's that got to do with it?'

Nan went pink. 'Well, when people talk about a man chasing girls it's not very nice. I think it means kissing and cuddling and – and all that, so I don't think I should mention it again if I were you. It might upset Grannie.'

Secretly I thought it sounded a friendly game and not in the least wicked. But then I remembered how bristly Grandpapa's moustache felt against my cheek and decided I mightn't enjoy it much after all.

Aunt Clare bought herself a tin trunk the very next day and brought it back with her in a taxi. But she upset Nan because she had the cabbie carry it upstairs and put it right in the middle of our Nursery so that we could hardly move, even though there was only one bed there now.

'It'll save your legs, Nan,' she explained. 'I'll bring all my things and put them on Diana's bed ready for packing as I sort them out.'

But because her diet hadn't worked very well and she was nervous anyway, Aunt Clare kept changing her mind, so my bed was permanently piled up either with things she'd just thought of or things she'd changed her mind about and asked Nan to unpack again.

'More nuisance than she was over that concert,' grumbled poor Nan. 'Thank goodness it'll be out of our way on Saturday. Three times I've folded that pink georgette in layers of tissue and three times she's had it out again. I don't know what's got into her, I really don't.'

So, on Thursday afternoon, Grannie said Nan and I could go and see about my uniform and have tea at the Fuller's in Buckingham Palace Road as a treat. I think she was looking forward to Aunt Clare going away, too, because every time I heard them together Aunt Clare was telling Grannie all the things she mustn't do and mustn't let me do once she'd gone.

It was November but that Thursday afternoon was so warm and sunny Nan and I thought it would be lovely to walk across Green Park to Gorringes instead of going all the way by bus. It was a Park we hardly ever went to and it was so empty it was just like being in the country. I never actually said so, but Nan seemed to know I was still frightened of walking on grass after McRawley because we always kept to the paths now. We had nearly got as far as Buckingham Palace when a tall, thin young man dressed all in black came walking slowly towards us. He was very, very handsome and he was carrying a single dark-red rose.

'Nan,' I whispered. 'Do you think he's the Prince of Wales?'

'No, he's far too tall – and the Prince of Wales is fair.'

I couldn't stop staring at him as he got nearer because the next time I did Jenny and Mr Anstruther's story I was going to make Mr Anstruther look exactly like him. I didn't realize that he must have been staring at me, too, until he stopped in front of us and held out the rose.

'Big brown eyes,' he murmured, bending down to have another look in case mine were blue after all but they weren't. 'My heart has just been broken by eyes like yours, so please, take the flower she spurned and treat your lovers more gently when you grow up.'

'Oh, I *will*,' I promised, quite carried away. It was like being in a story. 'Thank you.'

He pushed the rose at me so quickly I dropped it, but he walked straight on past us without looking back.

'*Well!*' Nan gasped. 'The poor young man must be cranky. It can't be sunstroke, not at this time of year!'

I picked up the flower feeling, just for a moment, tall and beautiful like Jenny. Then the thorns pricked my hand and I said: 'But how am I going to carry it shopping? It's so long and prickly?'

There was a seat a little further on, so we sat down and Nan fished in her handbag until she found her little nail-scissors shaped like a stork with a long beak, and a clean hanky.

'We haven't a vase tall enough anyway,' she said, 'so if I cut the stalk down and wrap it up carefully, I think it should last all right laid on top of my purse.'

We soon forgot the young man and the rose when we got to the school uniform department in Gorringes, though. Nan had the clothes list that 'Glen Coe' had sent us and we couldn't get over how pretty the things were – or how many I must have all at once.

'And every single thing with a name-tape to be sewn on,' said Nan. 'I'll be sewing from now till you go!'

By the time we got home after a lovely tea at Fuller's with their special walnut cake, the red rose had wilted pretty badly but it was still a beautiful colour.

'Shall we press it in our Bible like we did the four-leaf clover?' said Nan.

'Oh, *yes*. Then it can live forever and ever in the shoe-box with your plaits, can't it? I can take the box to school, can't I?'

Nan thought for a bit, then she shook her head. 'Better not, darling. The other children mightn't understand. It'll be safe here for you every holidays. I think you'd best take your little Teddies and the fluffy dog Grannie gave you last Christmas, that way you'll be like all the others.'

If we were all going to be dressed alike and have the same toys I wanted to ask Nan if she thought we'd all end up looking alike, too, but Aunt Clare came in just then in a dreadful temper, carrying four of her new dresses.

'It's no good, they still don't fit! I've got absolutely nothing to wear and I don't think I shall go to rotten Hong-Kong at all!'

Nan took the dresses from her and began to fold them expertly on my bed.

'Now, now, Miss Clare. As soon as you get to really hot Foreign Parts you'll lose weight in a jiffy, your Aunt Felicity said she lost a whole stone as soon as she went to India. You take a nice aspirin when you go to bed and things'll look much better tomorrow.'

The Nursery felt almost as big as the drawing-room when she and her trunk finally left on Saturday.

Great-Uncle Vincent was exactly like the drawings of Mr Pickwick except that his face was brown and he had bandy legs. I didn't think he'd be able to chase girls to kiss and cuddle any more, because his tummy was so fat he'd never get near their faces. But his bright blue eyes twinkled and wrinkled up with laughter so often that they almost disappeared, and he wasn't the least like Grannie or any of her brothers and sisters. I liked him straight away.

He arrived on Friday at lunch-time when there was only Grannie and me, and I knew she must love him very much because she looked beautiful again, instead of pale and ill, and as soon as Charlesworth showed him up to the drawing-room she held out her arms and said:

'Oh, *Vin* – my dear. Thirty years has been so long. How are you?'

He kissed both her hands and kept holding them while he looked at her.

'I'm fat, prosperous – and sick of sheep for the moment! But you, Elizabeth, I hear you haven't been too well?'

'Rubbish!' Grannie sounded brisk and kept on smiling at him. 'It's a plot to hide me away, the way we used to hide you when Father was furious, do you remember?'

I felt they ought to be alone and tried to tip-toe out and wait on the stairs until the gong went, but I bumped into a little table and Grannie saw me.

'Don't go away, darling. Come and meet your Great-Uncle Vincent.' And to him she explained: 'This is Diana, Georgina's daughter; though Matthew and I feel she really belongs to us, now.'

It was such a lovely thing for her to say that I ran back and kissed her cheek before turning to hold out my hand. But Great-Uncle Vincent didn't take it, instead he squatted down on his crooked legs so that our faces were level.

'It's a pleasure to meet you, Diana. You and I are going to be mates, eh? So let's drop some of the trimmings. You call me "Uncle Vin", not half such a mouthful.'

For the first time I realized that he talked differently to us, his 'a's' were long and flat and his sentences went up at the end like singing.

'I'd like that, Uncle Vin. And I like you, too!'

He had to hold the arm of Grannie's chair to push himself up again, but he was very pleased and pulled something out of his waistcoat pocket with two fingers.

'A little bird told me you'd be here. This is good Australian gold and don't you forget it!'

He held out a beautiful gold coin and Grannie said:

'Oh, Vin! You're spoiling her already! Just the way you used to spoil us.'

'Why not? Spoiling is what pretty girls are for.'

The coin lay gleaming in my hand and 'Thank you very much' sounded dull and stupid after such a magnificent present. But Uncle Vin went on:

'Strikes me you're the only one young enough left to show me London, Diana – and I can afford the cab fares – so right off tomorrow we'll go and find a jeweller who'll fit that into a bracelet for you.'

'Can Nan come too?' I asked quickly, not wanting her to miss a treat.

'Anyone you like,' he said, throwing out his fat arms as though he'd like to take the whole house.

After that he and Grannie talked mostly to each other,

but with the shining coin beside me on the dining-room table I ate up my fish and rice in record time, longing to tell Nan all that had happened.

It was a drizzly afternoon so Maisie and I didn't go for a walk. Instead, while Nan was helping Grannie into bed because the excitement of seeing Uncle Vin had given her a bad headache, I had time to go right through Jenny's story, changing Mr Anstruther into the dark, handsome young man with the rose. I thought about changing his name, too, but Jenny was so used to her happy ending as Mrs Anstruther I thought I'd better leave it. Then Nan brought our tea-pot up from the bathroom and we settled down by the fire to make toast. Suddenly there was a tap on the door and Uncle Vin came in carrying a white paper bag.

'May I join you? I've brought some rations and I can't stand that big room downstairs on my own. Back home we usually sit down thirty or forty of us to meals.' Nan stood up and he pumped her hand up and down, beaming. 'You must be the famous "Nan" I've been hearing about. My goodness,' he looked at us both, 'one could put the pair of you in a pint pot and there'd still be room to spare! You need feeding up.'

He opened his paper bag, peered at our table, and put three brown macaroons and three chocolate éclairs on the plate with our two coconut pyramids.

'Oh, Mr Vincent, Diana mustn't eat things like that!' Nan's face was red with embarrassment. 'She has to be ever so careful and the least thing makes her sick.'

'Sick?' He sat down in Nan's rocking-chair, making it creak, and pulled me towards him. I still liked him and I longed to taste a macaroon, but I knew Nan wasn't happy and his being there made the Nursery feel as if it was stuffed full of eiderdown. 'I can teach you a way to stop being sick, it's all in your breathing. Watch!'

He breathed in so deeply and held it so long his face

went mauve and his tummy looked even larger. Then he let it out slowly.

'Do that two or three times when you feel squeamish and you'll never be sick again. Now – you try.' He prodded my diaphragm with a podgy finger until I began to cough instead of breathing properly. Nan said:

'She's better with her grey powders, Mr Vincent. But you're welcome to a cup of tea if you'd like one?'

He stood up, heaving himself out of the rocking-chair with some difficulty. His eyes weren't twinkling any more, they looked small and sad.

'Tea?' he said. 'Think I'll go down to the dining-room and find something a bit stronger before my brother-in-law gets home.' He looked from me to Nan and mumbled something that sounded like: 'Didn't mean to intrude . . . thought my new little mate deserved a treat, that's all.' And he lumbered out.

'Oh, Nan – should I run down with him? He looks so lonely.'

'No, darling. I'll have to talk to Grannie first. We aren't used to gentlemen coming up here and . . .' She looked at the rich, expensive cakes on the table. 'We can't have him making you ill again, not so soon before Christmas.'

'But couldn't I just *taste* a macaroon? It'll be years and years before I'm twelve, and Aunt Clare need never know.'

Nan hesitated, then she smiled. 'We'll have half each,' she said. 'Then, if it doesn't upset you you shall have a whole one tomorrow. I'd forgotten it was your Aunt Clare said they'd be bad for you.'

She cut it carefully, giving me the part with the almond on, and I took tiny bites to make it last, trying to chew each one a hundred times, only they were gone by the time I'd counted to thirty. The soft, nutty flavour was so delicious I prayed that I wouldn't be sick so that I could taste it again.

I wasn't. But Grannie and Grandpapa decided that Uncle Vin mustn't come to the Nursery any more, so for the rest of his two-week visit he hardly spoke to me at all. And we never went out in taxis to see London or have my gold coin put into a bracelet. Instead, Nan put it carefully in our treasure box, wrapped in cottonwool.

But on his last evening, before he left us to stay with Great-Uncle Joe, Grannie sent me down to the drawing-room to say goodbye because he'd be starting very early in the morning. She was resting to make sure she'd feel well enough to go down for dinner.

Uncle Vin didn't see me at first. He was walking round the room, his hands behind his back, peering at all the photographs. I was sure he hadn't noticed me – so I jumped when he asked, without turning round :

'Is this your mother, Diana ?'

'Yes.'

'H'm. Pretty, isn't she ? She wasn't even born when I went out to Australia. Why don't you live with her ?'

I had to think for a little while because I wasn't absolutely sure myself. Then I said : 'Well, I'm sick rather often and sometimes I can't help putting my tongue out and shrugging my shoulder. Like this.' I gave him a demonstration. 'And Mother got cross when her friends were there.'

Uncle Vin roared with laughter and slapped me so hard on the back I nearly fell over. 'Not got much sense of humour, eh ? Those tricks of yours would go down at any party in Australia, I can tell you. And if I had a little girl like you I'd want her with me all the time.'

'Haven't you got any children at all ?'

'No. Just a whole lot of sheep and some good mates. Mind you, when I got here I said I was sick of sheep but now I'm not so sure. They never let you down like people. I don't know that coming over here after all these years has been such a good idea. People change, they change a lot.'

'I expect you've changed, too. You must have been thin when you chased the girls.' I stopped, appalled at what I'd said, but it had just slipped out. Uncle Vin stared at me.

'My God,' he said very softly. 'Unto the third and fourth generation!' Then more loudly he asked : 'D'you mean they *still* tell that old story ?'

'Not really. And I'm very sorry if I hurt your feelings, Uncle Vin. I only heard Great-Aunt Gussie and Great-Aunt Madge saying something one day at lunch. That's all.'

'Would you like to know what happened?'

I shivered a little, knowing Grannie would want me to say 'No'. But none of the relations had ever talked to me properly before and it was very exciting, so I nodded.

Uncle Vin sat down on the sofa and patted the place beside him.

'It's a very short, very sad story,' he began – most disappointingly. 'And I hope, when you've heard it, you'll always try to find out the truth of things for yourself and not believe everything you hear.'

'Yes, Uncle Vin.' It was only going to be a lecture after all, and I began to fidget, but a few seconds later I was spellbound.

'When we were young your Grannie and I and all our brothers and sisters lived in a big house in the country. I came somewhere about the middle of the family, I suppose – anyway, I was twenty when this story happened and your Great-Aunt Felicity wasn't much bigger than you. Our parents were very strict, especially Father. I wanted to be a farmer and he'd made up his mind I was to go into the Church. I wasn't one for preachifying – though he made me go to College to study for it, mind. No, I liked being out of doors and pretty girls and parties . . . my word, we had some magnificent picnic parties, sometimes as many as fifty of us if we were all home and our friends joined in! We'd start by the river, then off to the woods for a spot of slap and tickle . . . *errrhm!*' Uncle Vin cleared his throat loudly, hoped I hadn't heard and quickly substituted: 'A spot of hide-and-seek. Wonderful the girls looked in their summer dresses and big hats with ribbons – and we lads very much The Thing in our bow-ties and white flannels . . .' He paused, seeing it all again, and I could see it too until he said: 'Would you believe it, old Gussie was a real beauty in those days! Yes, even better looking than Elizabeth . . .'

He was forgetting the story and I did want to hear it before anyone came in, so I said:

'Please get to the bit where you were packed off to Australia, Uncle Vin. I *do* want to hear it.'

'Eh?' He came slowly out of the woods, looked down at me and remembered where we were. 'Oh. Yes. Well, you see, I fell in love . . . not with any of my sisters' friends, though. No, my Betsy was a maid like your whatsername here, Charlesworth.'

'But not with chronic feet?' I gasped.

'Good lord, no. Lovely as an angel, she was, and only seventeen.' It was all right, she was going to turn out just like Jenny. Only she didn't. 'Clouds of black curly hair she had, and big brown eyes like, like saucers.' Emotion had made him run out of poetry so he blew his nose very hard. 'I knew my family would never allow us to marry, and we were both under age, so we planned to run away . . .'

I was breathing so hard I was afraid I'd interrupted him, but he'd forgotten me again. 'Father caught me coming out of her room,' he said. And stopped. I waited until I couldn't bear the suspense any longer.

'And what happened next, Uncle Vin?'

'Next?' He looked down at me vaguely. 'Nothing. Mother sent Betsy straight back to her family, and Father packed me off to Australia.'

I'd never felt so let down in my life – not even when Nan told me Aunt Clare hadn't bothered to find out if her poetic French Count had been run over by a bus.

'But when you love someone, how *can* you just let them be sent away and be sent away yourself? Didn't you try and follow her or – or do something?' I could see poor Betsy so clearly, with her eyes like saucers staring and staring out of a poor little window while her face got thinner and thinner and Uncle Vin never came. I stood up and looked at his fat face. 'If someone sent Nan away I'd keep looking for her till I died,' I said, and ran out of the drawing-room before the tears came.

Grannie told me later that I seemed to have upset Uncle Vin and she hoped I hadn't put my tongue out. I promised

I hadn't – except in fun to show him – and I couldn't explain. Love *must* matter more than Aunt Clare and Uncle Vin made out. If it didn't, I couldn't see the point of growing up and getting married at all.

PART SIX

Christmas was very quiet that year with nearly all the
Great-Aunts and -Uncles back in India and Hong-Kong. Even
Great-Aunt Alicia and Great-Uncle Joe were away, as they'd
taken Uncle Vin to see someone called Aunt Pussy in Bath.
She was Great-Grandfather's youngest sister, and so old

Grannie thought she might be a hundred. From there Uncle Vin was going back to Australia. It had worried me so much I couldn't help asking Grannie:

'Isn't Uncle Vin going to try and find Betsy, the lovely maid you had with black curly hair that he fell in love with?'

'Betsy?' Grannie thought hard, drawing her eyebrows together, then she shook her head. 'We never had a maid with that name, and certainly never one with black hair. I'd remember because, as the eldest daughter, I helped my mother to run the house. No, Uncle Vin was very charming when he was young, but I'm afraid he was a bit of a Bad Hat altogether.'

So his lecture and his sad story with the poor ending had been lies. At first I was angry with him, and then I thought of Jenny and Mr Anstruther; they were as real to me as Nan or Grannie, even though Mr Anstruther had lost his tall hat and sponge-bag trousers recently, turning into the beautiful, dark young man in black. I suddenly wished that I could see Uncle Vin again. If Betsy was a person he'd made up to comfort himself, I would have told him about Jenny and we might have become real friends.

In spite of being quiet, that Christmas Day was very cosy. At lunch there were only Grannie, Grandpapa, Great-Aunt Gussie, Great-Aunt Fidge and me. There was so much room round the table that Great-Aunt Fidge felt quite safe and even told us a funny story about an old rag-and-bone man with a barrow. She got rather muddled and I don't think any of us understood quite what he had done, but we were so glad she was happy that we laughed and laughed.

When it was time to open our presents Grannie asked Nan to stay in the drawing-room, which made everything nicer still. Because I was going away to school my presents were very grown-up, in small, exciting parcels: a silver wristwatch from Grannie and Grandpapa, an Eversharp pencil from Great-Aunt Gussie, and Great-Aunt Fidge gave me six white hankies with 'D' embroidered in the corner. Mother and Daddy sent another brooch, but instead of something balanced on the end, this one had three small diamonds right along the middle. Nan pinned it across my collar and it flashed and sparkled every time I looked in the tall mirror. Then, before Nan and I went up to the Nursery, Grannie said:

'As you're nearly a grown-up schoolgirl now, Diana, I wondered if we should have a small birthday tea-party for you before you go away? You could ask your friend Deborah Watson-Leigh and her Nanny if you like.'

'You mean a real tea-party *here*, in the drawing-room?' I only just stopped my shoulder flying up with excitement as Grannie nodded, smiling. Then I hugged her very hard. I didn't even ask her who would be coming, it was so wonderful that I was to have Deborah to tea for the first time.

The tea-party was fixed for three days before school started. Grannie and Nan had decided this together because, even if it brought on a bilious attack, I should be well enough to catch the school train.

'Who's going to come?' I asked Nan. I'm not sure what I was expecting, really, but the word 'party' sounded gay and special. Perhaps some of the cousins I'd never seen would be invited up from the country. But Nan looked worried.

'Now, darling, don't go getting over-excited, will you? Grannie is too delicate to stand a lot of noise and she *is* letting you have Deborah. I think she's just asked the aunts and uncles – oh, and that nice Mr Pender and his new wife from the choir. You like him, don't you? And it seemed a good chance, Grannie thought, while Aunt Clare is away.'

'Mrs Pender'll only suck acid-drops. And her voice wobbles.' It was a babyish, petty thing to say, like kicking the leg of a table in a tantrum. I was sorry at once.

'I didn't mean to be horrid, Nan, it's only that I'd like there to be some smart people for Deborah to see . . . *new* people as it's a party.'

Nan put her arm round me.

'I know, I know. But try and think of it this way – all the Aunts and Uncles are very fond of you, even Great-Aunt Gussie in her own way. I'm sure a tea-party is

Grannie's way of wishing you good luck at "Glen Coe" and they all want to be part of it. Deborah won't mind. I've suggested that you and she should have a special table to yourselves by the piano, so you can laugh and talk as much as you like. And when you get to the school, remember, all the girls will be new and interesting. Why, by this time next year you'll have more friends than you know what to do with!'

I didn't make friends easily, and for the last few nights I'd lain in bed wishing I needn't go to 'Glen Coe' among so many strangers. I was afraid that Deborah, who was pretty and popular, wouldn't want me as her best friend any more, either. But something else Nan had just said was more important at the moment.

'Won't you and Nanny Warriss be with us in the drawing-room?'

'Good gracious no, darling. That wouldn't be right at all!' She was shocked at the very idea. 'We shall have our tea up here and wait till Grannie rings the bell for you two to be fetched.'

For the first time in my life I wished that Mother was going to be there; at least Deborah would think her smart and beautiful. In our quiet, remote Nursery world it had never occurred to me to wonder how anyone outside would see my relations. Nobody from outside ever came, and Nan and I were so used to them all: Great-Aunt Gussie's booming, Great-Aunt Fidge with her veils and gloves and Great-Uncle Joe's winking eye. But Deborah, used to her light, white house, her own pink bath and her mother's drawing-room filled with chic, gay people . . . Would she, *could* she, laugh at mine?

Once there, the idea tormented me. In fact I was torn in half because I didn't want to be ill and make dear Nan over-tired again, but I did, desperately, want to be ill enough not to have Deborah at the tea-party. The struggle between the two produced one of my flickery, sick head-aches but when I saw Nan's anxious face I remembered Uncle Vin and his breathing-not-to-be-sick. I tried it and it really worked. I only wished I could have told him before he went back to Australia – it would have made up to him a little for me not understanding that his Betsy was as important to him as Jenny was to me.

Three days before the tea-party my school uniform arrived from Gorringes, and a new trunk with my long name printed right across the top in black was already on the landing outside the Nursery. One shelf of our cupboard was piled up with all the blouses, nighties, knickers and socks that Nan had sewn name-tapes in, but Gorringes embroidered each girl's initials in the dresses, smocks and saxe-blue overcoat. The problem was, where could we hang them all? There were only four pegs behind our chintz curtain and those were full with our everyday things.

In the end Grannie said we'd better use Aunt Clare's wardrobe as it was half empty. I was afraid my lovely new clothes would smell of her scent, but it had all gone and the room only smelt deserted.

On the morning before the tea-party I clung to Nan and sobbed out everything: how much I dreaded going away to school, and how frightened I was that Deborah might laugh at the family and not be my friend any more.

Nan wrung out a flannel in cold water and laid it over my hot, throbbing eyes, then, as I sat curled up on the floor by her chair, she began gently brushing my hair that had somehow got hot and damp as well.

'Darling, you have to go on in life; everybody has to. It isn't right for you to spend all your time with old people any longer. You've already learnt how to be brave during that time in Devon. Now it's time you learnt to be young . . . Oh, I know you are, darling, you're still almost a baby really, but you need to get up to mischief a bit, make some noise now and then. Although, mind you're not naughty, now! That's not what I mean at all.'

'And what about Deborah?' I asked, my voice still rather croaky.

'All I can say is that if Deborah Watson-Leigh laughs at

our family then she's no friend worth having!' And Nan started to brush my hair much more briskly.

It rained on the day of the party so, as Maisie and I couldn't go out, Charlesworth let me help her set the tea.

'It'll be quiet here without you, Miss Diana,' Charlesworth said, hobbling upstairs with a big tray of plates, cups and saucers. I was behind her, carrying a tall cake-stand very carefully because it had a pink iced sponge on it that smelt deliciously of pear drops.

'I don't think I make much noise,' I pointed out.

'No, but it's nice having a young face about the place.'

We had to make five more journeys before everything was ready except for the big silver tea-pot and matching kettle that stood on a spirit lamp, and they would only arrive when all the visitors had come. Charlesworth put a special, big plate of mixed Fancies, chocolate biscuits and, joy of joys, two macaroons on the small table set for Deborah and me. Then it was time for me to go upstairs and get tidy.

All my fears came back, only a hundred times worse.

'If I'm sick would Deborah and Nanny Warriss have to go home again?' I asked Nan hopefully.

'No. And you know you aren't going to be sick, Diana,' Nan said very firmly. 'You're beginning to grow out of all that now, thank goodness, and just think how upset Grannie would be if you weren't there. She's arranged the afternoon specially for you.'

So we went down to the hall to wait for Deborah so that I could take her up to the drawing-room myself.

Great-Aunt Gussie arrived first, shaking the raindrops off herself like a large, tweed dog, although she'd only walked from her cab to the front door.

'My God, what a day,' she said, letting Charlesworth help her off with her Burberry. Suddenly I plucked up courage and walked out of the dining-room door where Nan and I were standing.

'Hello, Great-Aunt Gussie.'

'H'm.' She looked down at me, then pulled a ten-shilling

My trunk was ready in the hall and my new attaché case, a present from Grannie, was beside it. Inside, it had a packet of pale blue writing-paper and envelopes, tied up with dark blue ribbon, a book of stamps, two of my little Teddy-bears and a pound of assorted toffees. Each girl, it said in the prospectus, should take a pound of sweets to go into the big tins handed round to the whole school every day after lunch, when each girl was allowed to take two.

I'd woken up very early that morning and moved about quietly so as not to wake Nan next door. Nan had fixed her two grey plaits on to a band of elastic for me, so I opened the shoe-box and put those on my head first. Then I went round the Nursery looking at everything slowly and carefully so that I'd be able to see them all any time that I closed my eyes. Actually, I stared at our red cloth on the table for too long because the bobbles round the edge started jigging about.

Then Nan came in in her dressing-gown and the hair-net she wore in bed to keep her short hair tidy.

'Whatever are you doing, darling? I hoped you'd sleep on a bit.'

'I couldn't, Nan.'

'Tell you what, then. I'm just going down to make my cup of tea, would you like one too?'

I said yes, please, and in five minutes we were sitting side by side on my bed drinking it. I was still wearing her plaits, although I was so used to her short white hair now it was hard, sometimes, to remember how she'd looked with a darkish grey bun. I said:

'You won't change any more, will you, Nan? Promise?'

She laughed. 'I don't expect so. You're the one who'll be changing all the time now as you grow up.'

'I don't want to grow up,' I said passionately, terrified again at the thought of all the strange girls and going in a train without Nan. 'I'd like to go back to – to the Christmas when Great-Aunt Madge gave me Betsy Caroline and then stay like that with you for always.'

'Come on,' Nan said gently. 'Let's get you dressed in your smart new uniform so that you can show Grannie and Grandpapa at breakfast.'

The saxe-blue serge dress with a pale blue silk collar embroidered with 'G.C.' in each corner *was* smart, and Nan had made Alice-bands to keep my hair neatly back so that my ears wouldn't stick through.

'Well, well.' Grandpapa smiled as I went into the dining-room. 'We've got a Princess for breakfast, I see!' And after Prayers he gave me a crisp, new pound note. 'A Princess must have plenty of pocket money,' he said.

After he'd gone off in his tall silk hat to the office,

Grannie and I sat in the dining-room waiting for my taxi to arrive.

The dreadful thing was, we couldn't think of anything to say.

'I know you'll be happy – but if you're not you will write and tell us, won't you, darling?' she said two or three times.

And once I said: 'I promise I'll be happy. In fact I may not even want to come back for holidays!' I'd meant it to comfort her, but it came out all wrong and hurt her feelings.

Then Charlesworth creaked in in her new shoes to say the taxi was ready and Nan was in the hall.

I clung to Grannie, getting my hair mixed up with her long pearls, trying to say all the things that wouldn't come before – especially making her promise faithfully not to die. That made me cry and she pushed me back very gently, saying:

'You mustn't cry, darling. Think if you got tears on your lovely new dress and look, here's Nan with your coat and hat. Let me see how they look.'

When we got into the hall Charlesworth was standing there with tears trickling down her big, bony cheeks.

'Now just you take care and be a good girl, Miss Diana,' she said, almost as if she was angry. 'And here – it's not much, but I made it, and Petty and I hope it'll bring you ever such good luck.'

It was a dear little gollywog made from red, black and blue darning wool. But when I looked up to thank her Charlesworth was disappearing through the baize door.

I put the gollywog in my pocket and Nan said:

'Come on, darling. I've thought of a splendid way to pass the taxi ride.'

As soon as our cabbie slammed the door and started his engine Nan opened her handbag and brought out our playing cards.

'I thought we'd play Snap,' she said.

We balanced my attaché case on our knees, but every

time the taxi turned a corner all the cards slid off and we ended up laughing so much that we arrived at Victoria in no time.

But I think we both knew nothing would ever be quite the same again.